THE DARWEN COUNTY
HISTORY SERIES

A History of
DEVON

Map of modern Devon

A History of
DEVON

Robin Stanes

Drawings by Jim Stanes and Judy Stevens
Cartography by Jim Stanes

Phillimore

2000

Published by
PHILLIMORE & CO. LTD.
Shopwyke Manor Barn, Chichester, West Sussex

First published 1986
Second edition, 2000

ISBN 1 86077 092 4

Printed and bound in Great Britain by
BUTLER AND TANNER LTD.
London and Frome

Contents

For Clemency after fifty years together in Devon;
for James, Lucy, Alex, Jessica and Carey who were all born here,
and once again for Dick Wills of Ilsington and Brian Clist of Hemyock,
Devon farmers, the fourteenth and twelfth generations, respectively,
of their families to have lived in those places.
Their forbears must have seen it all.

List of Illustrations

Frontispiece: Map of modern Devon

List of Colour Illustrations

List of Illustration Acknowledgements

The author is grateful for permission to reproduce the following plates: H.M. The Queen, 70; Royal Commission on Historical Monuments (England), National Monuments Record, Air Photo Unit, 5, 74; Cambridge University Collection, 13, 18, 45; Nicholas Horne Ltd., 38, 57, 61, 94, 113, 117, 131, 132, 144; F.M. Griffith, 55; Mike Benson (Photography), 47, 50, 135; Castle Photographers, Tiverton, 60, 63, 77; Devon County Council, 42; Barrie Aughton, Newquay, 73; Christopher J. Wormald, A.I.I.P., 78, 107; Martin Street Photography, Honiton, 66, 79; National Portrait Gallery, 100, 101, 108; the National Trust, V, VI, VIII; National Maritime Museum, 140; Dartmoor National Park, I-IV; Royal Institution of Cornwall, Truro, 128; Charles Hulland, 95; Jim Stanes, 40, 59, 86, 111, 116, 123; Ben Du Buisson, 33, 54, 93, 96; Torquay Museum, endpapers, XI, 129, 139, 156, 157; the Earl of Devon, VII; *Western Morning News*, 138, IX; Plymouth Local Studies Library, 141; Plymouth Art Gallery, X; Mrs. B. Johns, 82; Still Images, XII-XIV; Robin Stanes, 58, 64, 65, 67, 84, 105, 110, 124-7, 134, 142, 143, 148, 154, 155.

Acknowledgements to the First Edition

Local historians must be jacks of all trades; the inevitable corollary must follow, I suppose. Nevertheless, I hope that I have neither perpetuated nor created any myths. This book is really the result of the work I have done over the last years for the Extra Mural Department of the University of Exeter, lecturing on the history of the county. Bob Pim launched me on that work, and to him I owe a considerable debt. I also owe a great debt to the members of my Extra Mural classes, who have taught me so much. No-one could write a word about the history of Devon without being in considerable debt to (the late) Professor W.G. Hoskins.

Many people have helped me with this book. Henrietta Quinnell, of the Extra Mural Department, guided my hand with the first two chapters; Stephen Fisher, Brian Clapp, the late Walter Minchinton, all of Exeter University, and Harold Fox of the University of Leicester, read certain chapters and I have mostly, but not always, taken their advice. Greg Finch, once a pupil, helped me immensely with the chapter on the 19th century; I have consulted his doctoral thesis, and those of Robert Whiting, Tom Greaves and R.A. Higham, with profit, and I hope that I have interpreted their findings correctly; any errors are mine alone.

I must also mention Brian Clist, Anne Glyn Jones, the late Elizabeth Gawne, Peter Hunt, (the late) Charles Hulland, Ian Maxted, Ian Mercer, (the late) Geoffrey Paley, (the late) Jeffrey Porter, John Pike, Bob Silvester, Sheila Stirling, Freda Wilkinson, Dick Wills and (the late) John Yallop, who all gave me help and advice. The staff of the Devon Record Office have also helped me, as have other folk too numerous to mention. Frances Griffith of the Devon County Property Department helped me immensely with finding the appropriate aerial photographs, some of which she took herself; her extensive collection of aerial photographs of the county must shed much new light on its pre-history. My son James did all the maps except one, and he and Judy Stevens did all the marginal drawings, some of which were based on the unpublished notebooks of Peter Orlando Hutchinson, by permission of the Devon Record Office. The map of Domesday Devon is reproduced from *The Domesday Geography of South-Western England* by H.C. Darby and R. Welldon Finn and is reproduced by permission of the Syndics of the Cambridge University Press.

The Governors of Exmouth School and Devon County Education Committee gave me a term's unpaid leave of absence to write part of the book; and my editors have encouraged, criticised, pressed and been patient. Judith Adam and Terry Hampson have typed from my untidy script. Above all, my wife has encouraged, supported, and helped me, and suffered a good deal of domestic disruption.

ROBIN STANES

Payhembury and Appledore
December, 1985

Preface and Acknowledgements to the Second Edition

In the 14 years that have elapsed since this book was first published much work has been done on the history of the county. Two large-scale collaborative works, on the *Maritime History of Devon* and *An Atlas of South Western History*, have been produced by the University. They have made a massive contribution to the history of the county.

More particularly, Mark Stoyle has revealed in his *Loyalty and Locality* the clear geography of the divided loyalty of the county in the Civil War and shown the resultant extent of destruction. Todd Gray has edited the household accounts of four Devonshire gentry and noble families in the 17th century and opened a new vista, that of the history of gardens in the county in *Devon's Garden History*. He has also edited the delightfully illustrated Swete's diary in four volumes as *Travels in Georgian Devon*. Bridget Cherry has updated and enlarged Pevsner's *Devon* and Peter Beacham and Peter Child have produced in *Devon Buildings* a finely illustrated description of Devon's old houses and their development. Della Hooke has edited a complete collection of the Anglo-Saxon charters of Devon.

Archaeologically the building of the new dual carriageway between Honiton and Exeter has revealed prehistoric settlement sites of many periods and probably fixed the location of the Roman settlement 'Moridunum', previously uncertain, at Pomeroy Wood, where a fort has been identified just east of Fenny Bridges. The foundations of the Roman road across the Axe were dramatically revealed by the building of the new Axminster by-pass. Jeremy Butler has produced in *An Atlas of Darmoor antiquities*, a survey, in five volumes, of relics of the past in that well used 'wilderness'.

Finally, I reiterate my thanks to those who helped me with the first edition and have enabled me to update and revise my work for this new edition.

ROBIN STANES

July, 2000

Introduction

Be they never so well mounted on their fine and dainty horses out of other counties, having travelled but one day's journey in this county, they will forbear the second

John Hooker, *Synopsis Chorographical of Devon*, 1600

For much of the past Devon has been rather on the periphery of English history. It was inaccessible, its roads appalling, as John Hooker's words indicate. Even by 1760 there was 'scarce a pair of wheels in the county'. Its boundaries, the sea to north and south, Celtic Cornwall to the west, and the narrow hilly waist of the south-western peninsula to the east, isolated it from the rest of the country.

This isolation contributed greatly to its history. Devon had an identity and an economy of its own, with a distinct rural culture; its own acre, its own hedged landscape, its own breeds of cattle and sheep, its own dialect and vocabulary, its own husbandry practices and even its own food—cider, pasties and cream. Local people seem to have been aware of this isolation and perhaps prided themselves on it. One 18th-century writer said that there was 'no thoroughfare' in Devon and that people were 'more stationary on one spot' and intermarried amongst themselves. Visitors to the county wrote about it rather as if it was a foreign land. This sense of separation and identity had political consequences. Devonshire people did not feel that their interests or wishes were necessarily best served by the government in London, and on occasion showed this clearly and dramatically.

Geography has made other contributions to the history and economy of the county. The two long coastlines of Devon, and its numerous harbours, have provided opportunities for trade, exploration, adventure, emigration, fishing, piracy, smuggling, and more lately for the holiday business, denied on such a scale to other counties. The geology of the county—the old rocks, the sharp and abrupt relief, the hills and valleys and the rivers and streams to which they give rise—provided power in abundance for industry before the invention of the steam engine. The damp, warm climate provided plentiful grazing for much of the year. From these—water power and wool—the Devon cloth industry grew. Further, the great volcanic upthrust of Dartmoor created veins of minerals in nearly all parts of the county, so that mining was at times almost as important a part of the economic life of the county as clothmaking.

Perhaps as a result of isolation, Devon was slow to adopt new ways and tended to cling to old ones. At the time of Domesday Book, Devon had far fewer water mills than counties further east, though this deficiency

1 *Exe Bridge at Exeter.*

2 *Tree cruck in the 'Treeroom', Pillavin, Witheridge.*

was soon to be remedied. Much later, the technology of the Industrial Revolution seems to have been ignored in the county until too late. In another context, Exeter saw the last burning of witches in the country, and one 18th-century Devonshire squire still kept a 'fool' to entertain his guests. Local society was old-fashioned at that time; Fielding's Squire Western, who lived in the 'old way', was a West Country man. Some new ideas were even resisted violently: political isolation and disenchantment showed its head in moments of crisis. The new ideas of the Reformation were one major cause, at least, of the Prayer Book Rebellion of 1549. In the next century, the Civil War found the West Country a centre of military activity, largely because of the attitude of the townspeople, who by and large disliked Charles I's government. They held out persistently for parliament and thus attracted the continuous attention of royalist armies. Forty years later, both the Duke of Monmouth and William of Orange chose to land in the West Country, believing that local folk were still 'agin the government', and needing a safe, remote base from which to operate. The 16th and 17th centuries were a period of turmoil and commotion for Devonshire people. Hardly a generation passed without a stir or disturbance of some sort, about which they had to make up their minds.

For other reasons as well these two centuries were the most remarkable and interesting in Devon's history. They saw the development and growth of a flourishing local economy, taking full advantage of the natural resources of the county. Tin mining and cloth making were at or approaching their peak of prosperity, and it could be argued that between 1500 and 1750 Devon was one of the most considerable industrial centres in the country, in the old 'domestic' sense.

Industry and the export trade went hand-in-hand. By the end of the 17th century, Devon's ships were trading with almost all the known world. Fishermen crossed the Atlantic to the Newfoundland banks, and settlers followed in their wake. Seaport towns grew in wealth, and Drake, Hawkins, Raleigh, Grenville and their followers drew on this well of experience and knowledge in their raids and voyages to the New World and beyond. At this point the thread of Devon's history is at one with national history.

By the 17th century Devonshire farming was sufficiently advanced to elicit the praise of Oliver Cromwell, himself a landowner. Without a prosperous agriculture the economy of the county would not have been soundly based. The abundance of hilly upland common land—relief and geology once again have their part to play in this—made for the early abandonment of the medieval open-field in favour of the enclosed farming landscape which is still more or less what is seen today. On these enclosed fields, Devonshire farmers practised their skills to good advantage, freed very largely from the rigidity of open-field farming, and it was doubtless this which attracted Cromwell's interest.

But the coming of the railway finally ended the isolation from which so much much of Devon's history stemmed. Tourism slowly took the place of trade and industry. Both mining and cloth-making declined and Devon's ships no longer exported Devon's goods in quantity, although there was still much shipping in the ports. Exeter, from being a great industrial city, became a cathedral 'service' town and all the political stirs and troubles were in the past. Devonshire farming was now thought to be old-fashioned, and from the rural areas of the county emigration took place on a vast scale, much of it overseas. The old rural life of Devon, a combination of farming and domestic industry, largely disappeared.

Thus the 19th century saw a great change in the character of the county. Its old distinct and particular nature, the product largely of geography and isolation, a contrary mixture of old-fashioned liking for old ways, a degree of political independence, and a thrusting go-ahead commercial enterprise, was largely lost. Devon became something of a rustic, sleepy backwater, a good place for the holidaymaker, a good place, indeed, to retire to. But this is not how it once was. For two or three centuries what John Hooker said of the county in 1600 was perhaps not so extravagant:

> And yet I know that all or most part of other provinces be rich and profitable and stored, some with corn and cattle, some with fruits, and some with sheep and wool, and some with one commodity or another. But yet generally they cannot compare so many as this little corner yieldeth in sundry respects, both for the public wealth and private profit, and specially for corn and cattle, for cloth and wool, for tin and metals, and for fish and sea commodities, all of which out of this county have passaged into all nations, and be very beneficial to the whole commonwealth.

3 *Blackborough miner trimming whetstones at the mouth of his mine, 1854.*

1

The Face of the County

Devon's boundaries are ancient, in part the product of geography, in part the result of conscious political decisions. To the east, from the sea near Lyme Regis, the boundary follows fairly closely the eastern edge of the Blackdown Hills to the neighbourhood of Bampton. Near Bampton the boundary swings north-west to leave, rather oddly, all Exmoor, the Quantocks and the Brendons in Somerset, until it reaches the sea again at Countisbury. Once, perhaps, all those hills lay within the boundaries of the ancient province and kingdom of Dumnonia.

To the west the Tamar is the boundary between Saxon Devon and Celtic Cornwall. King Aethelstan made it the boundary in the tenth century, and so it has remained, more or less, to the present day. To the south it was a good physical boundary, not easily crossed; along its whole length it had been, and still is to some extent, a racial, cultural and emotional one.

Within these boundaries there is great diversity. Devon is the third biggest county in England; it is 100 miles from Salcombe to Ilfracombe, and 70 from Axminster to the Tamar. It is the only English county with two separate coastlines, each with its own focus of trade and communications with foreign parts. In the past there were recognisable differences in dialect and vocabulary, and to some extent in the farming practices and economies of different parts of the county. Size and poor internal communications, differing soil and climate, all contributed to this diversity.

Physically, Dartmoor is the dominant feature. From it many of Devon's rivers radiate like the spokes of a wheel. Only the Tamar, the Exe, the Torridge, the East Devon and the Exmoor rivers rise elsewhere. Almost all of them run broadly north and south in deep valleys, right athwart the through roads. Between these valleys, warm and green and verdant, lie quite extensive stretches of tableland often windswept and thinly treed. Here, in the bleakest, highest parts, were furzy unenclosed commons and moors, now mostly cleared and drained. In the wider valleys lies much fertile meadowland, and every little stream once had its quota of grist or tucking mills. The estuaries of the rivers have been embanked and drained here and there.

4 *Haytor, Dartmoor.*

16

5 *A Bronze-Age settlement: fields and huts, with a parallel reave system at the top. Horridge Common, Dartmoor.*

Underlying the physical geography lies a distinct pattern of rocks. These, together with the climate, determine the nature of the soils, and these in turn have determined the settlement pattern, the farming, the prosperity and even in the past the land tenure of the different landscapes of the county.

Heavy rainfall and rotting granite have produced on Dartmoor a black, peaty, rocky soil, providing in historical times a scanty living for a few hardy farmers. In summer it was useful grazing ground for all the parishes next the moor, and for centuries tinners dug a precarious living from even the most desolate parts. Iron and copper and even silver were also mined, and the mines provided a useful summer occupation for the inhabitants of the towns and villages around the moor. As with other farming areas, Dartmoor had its own breed of sheep—the 'Dartmoor Whiteface'.

South of the moor lie the South Hams, a name of great antiquity, meaning, perhaps, 'the lands between the rivers, south of the moor'. Here the Devonian rocks have produced some of the kindest country in Devon with warm, pink, easily worked soil, and coastal valleys almost tropical in their luxuriance. This was and is good arable land, famous for its cider and barley, home of its own South Devon sheep and the huge South Hams cattle. These Devon rocks recur in the north of the county, but there they lie much higher and the climate is less kind. Exmoor, under-lain by these rocks, is as bleak as anywhere in Devon. Here on the edge of the moor at Molland the red North Devon breed of cattle is said to have originated, and the Exmoor Horn is the local sheep breed.

In between these Devonian outcrops, with Dartmoor intruding in the middle, are the 'Culm measures', cold clay soils in general, though very variable, sometimes unworkable in wet weather but always green in the driest summer, rainy and windswept, stretching almost from Bampton to Hartland and from South Molton to Tavistock and Chagford. Much of this land was poor rushy grazing ground in the past, perhaps once heavily wooded, the poorest land in the county, but much improved in recent years. Here towns and villages are fewer and tend to occupy the drier hilltop sites, in contrast to the valley locations in south and east Devon. The western parts of this area were the home of the Devon Longwool sheep.

Down the Exe valley and reaching as far south as Torbay, with an outlying finger as far as Hatherleigh, are the famous red soils of Devon, derived from the Permian sandstone. In general this is the best land in the county, thickly settled and heavily cultivated from the earliest times, good arable and meadowland with fine churches, prosperous farms, and grist, fulling and paper mills on the rivers.

Lastly, east of the Exe is found the high greensand plateau of east Devon, deeply cut by river valleys, in which most of the farms and villages lie. This was and is grassy dairying country, 'on the green side', its valley meadowlands immensely productive, its cheese and butter once sold far afield. East Devon became a great centre for cloth and lace making, and, for a time, for the growing of flax, with more than its share of small towns where industry and trade flourished.

Finally there is yet another distinct feature of the landscape, the sea coast, cliff-bound, rocky, with swift tides. Wherever the coast permitted, there were sea-going communities, with quays and shipyards and rope-walks. Cargoes were landed and fishing boats launched from open beaches and every river had its lime kilns by the 18th century. All Devon's ports—Plymouth, Exeter, Dartmouth, Teignmouth, Bideford and Barnstaple—had markets for farm produce, and an interest in the land to add to their many maritime activities.

Despite its size and diversity, Devon has rather surprisingly pre-served its identity. North Devon has always been 'different'; local folk claim a passport is necessary to visit it! It has its own capital at Barnstaple; another considerable port in Bideford; a base of fine farming land around the Taw and Torridge estuaries and its own local trade, focused on Wales, Ireland and the north of England, with links further afield with Virginia and Prince Edward Island. North Devon pottery, from the clay beds at Fremington and elsewhere, was exported to all parts of England

and to the New World, and there were other industries. Ilfracombe and Westward Ho! were both popular Victorian holiday resorts, both, at one time, with railway links. Kingsley, Kipling and Henry Williamson all found literary inspiration in this area, In any other geographical context, north Devon would be a separate county. If anything, it was (and perhaps still is) more remote and old-fashioned, more essentially Devon, than the rest of the county, although this quality will not, perhaps, outlive the new link road. See map.

Since the creation of the royal dockyard at Dock in the 18th century, Plymouth has had a rather separate history from the rest of the county. It was a base for the Channel fleet and an important part of the national defence of the country. For a time, it was a transatlantic liner port. It had far outgrown Exeter by 1801, and attained total administrative independence in 1914. Torbay, the focus of the Devon holiday industry, also became an independent borough in 1968. Both these towns were absorbed into the county of Devon in 1974 but became independent councils once more in 1998. These apart, the boundary lines and identity established over a thousand years ago remain virtually unchanged. Exeter, not Plymouth, is the capital of Devon, though the government and administration is largely in the hands of those born and bred outside the county.

6 *Dartmouth Castle and St Petrock's Church.*

2

Prehistory

Devon can hardly be said to have a prehistory of its own. The county boundaries do not seem to have been much of a hindrance to prehistoric man. The whole peninsula was open to influence and perhaps invasion from the sea, more readily so than much of the rest of the country. The result was a diversity of peoples and cultures, some with clear connections with the rest of the country, and some with obvious links across the seas. In contrast, the peninsula, and even the county, were large enough and divided enough by rivers, valleys and hills to create further diversity, so that there seems little overall uniformity in, for instance, burial customs, or in the building of hill-forts.

There are other considerations. A vast amount must have been destroyed by the plough in historic times, perhaps more so than in other counties, since it was old-established practice for Devon farmers to plough all ploughable land regularly and thoroughly, and even to plough and till unrewarding moorland. This, combined with a largely acid soil which destroys bones, has made the archaeologist's task difficult. Archaeological artefacts and finds thin out markedly once the Devon border is reached from the east. On Dartmoor, in contrast, structural remains are thick, and here the high moor has probably never been ploughed since the late Bronze Age. The wealth of remains may be an indication, even if it is not proof, of what has been destroyed elsewhere.

To begin at the beginning: the earliest remains in the county (almost in the whole country), dating from *c*.35,000 B.C., have been found in Kent's Cavern in Torquay. Devon was never covered by ice, never glaciated. The only visible remains of the Ice Age are what are known as 'erratics', boulders of no known Devon rock, deposited from ice floes drifting on to what is now the north coast of the county. Though not glaciated, the land can hardly have been habitable; but in the periods when the ice was in retreat, men established themselves in caves in the limestone in the south of the county. It was McEnery's excavations in the caves at Brixham and Torquay which finally proved, to an unbelieving Victorian public, that early man was contemporary with extinct animals.

Other caves—around Plymouth Sound, at Buckfastleigh, Chudleigh, and Torbryan—also contributed evidence of men of the Old Stone Age, and of the animals they hunted: the woolly rhinoceros, the mammoth, the hippopotamus, the straight-tusked elephant. Amongst the remains of these,

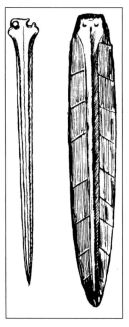

7 *Rapier blade and mould from Hennock.*

at the lowest level, were found crude hand-held axeheads of the earliest men. The gravel pits at Broom near Axminster were a source of a great many of these axes. Tornewton Cave, near Torbryan, which contains the best sequence of animal bones in the country, also gave evidence of the activities of Neanderthal man. Indications of his diet came from a conical pile of bones, crushed but preserved by a fall of rock, lying just where they had been carelessly discarded from a ledge on the cliff above, some 60,000 years ago. At the mouth of this cave, so obviously an 'entrance to the underworld', an unlicensed chapel was built in medieval times, perhaps to celebrate some pagan non-Christian ceremonies.

By the New Stone Age, the Neolithic, there is much more to be recognised, and a much greater population. Hembury, near Honiton, was the site of a 'causewayed camp', a banked enclosure inside a ditch, only partially dug, leaving causeways across it. Here a group of grain-growing, stock-rearing farmers lived in flimsy huts with thin defences, for some three to four centuries around 4,000 B.C. The site was abandoned and then reoccupied some three thousand years later by Iron-Age folk. On Haldon Hill, perhaps visible from Hembury, and on Hazard Hill near Totnes, there were similar largely undefended sites. At Hazard Hill there was a prolific flint industry, and on Beer Head in east Devon was another intensively settled flint working site. Mutters' Moor and High Peak near Sidmouth, and Bridford are other sites of this kind. Many more probably await discovery.

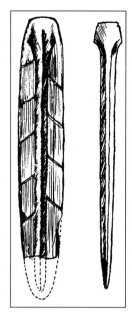

8 *Rapier blade and mould from Hennock.*

Roughly contemporary with these settlements, though difficult to interpret, are the communal graves of the south-west; the chambered tombs, passage graves and the 'shilstones' or shelfstones. All merit the name 'megalith', built as they were out of vast slabs of granite or other rocks. All of them seem to have been designed for successive communal burials; none of them are as large or dramatic as other examples in Ireland and Brittany. The best known shilstone is Spinster's Rock near Drewsteignton. This, like the others, probably originally covered with earth, had been denuded by Saxon times, since the name 'shilstone' is Saxon. Four shilstones survive in Devon, and another four have been destroyed but are commemorated by the farm-name 'Shilstone'. Field names might reveal more yet.

Towards the end of the Neolithic period (around 2000 B.C.), groups known to archaeologists as the Beaker people began to cross to Britain from Europe. They take their name from the characteristic red pots they produced. They were hunters familiar with the bow, but also farmers, who quickly established their authority over the earlier settlers of Neolithic times, and perhaps amalgamated with them. They differed from them in burying their dead alone under small round barrows, and they knew something of metallurgy, making copper knives and awls, though their sophisticated arrowheads were always flint. Relics of these people are thinly but widely spread in the south-west.

Traces of their religious rites have been discovered on what became eventually a holy site of great significance on Farway Common near

9   Bronze-Age shale cup, Broad Down, Farway.

Honiton. Some sixty barrows of rather late date have been located there, though the surrounding ridges and hill-tops are comparatively bare. On Dartmoor, Neolithic people may have been responsible for many of the familiar stone rows and avenues. These were perhaps ceremonial and commemorative, frequently leading to a small cairn or burial place. Other, much longer, stone rows, like the one on Stall Moor, two and a quarter miles long, may possibly have marked the site of some ceremonial games. The stone circles of Dartmoor and Bodmin Moor also seem, rather uncertainly, to date from the Beaker period. These were also ceremonial religious sites, built in a great variety of locations, some where any rites held within them could only be seen from afar. These people were probably also responsible for the standing stones, the 'menhirs' like Bear Down Man on Dartmoor or the Long Stone at Challacombe on Exmoor. One Cornish example (now destroyed) was 24 feet high. Again, their purpose is uncertain. It seems possible that the stone circles were set up using a local standard unit of measurement, a 'megalithic yard'.

Easier to understand, and to date, are the hut circles, pounds and round barrows of Dartmoor. They belong to what is known as the Bronze Age, when the technique of mixing tin with copper to produce a hard metal was developed, some time after 2,000 B.C. Barrows survive in considerable numbers on Dartmoor and Exmoor and other high ground. Their siting seems to indicate that these were important burial places, probably of chieftains, designed to be seen from afar. In all, some thousand or more have been identified in Devon, and there may once have been a great many more, destroyed when the tops of the hills were ploughed and cleared. Not all, however, were on hill-tops: there is a curiously sited group at Upton Pyne in the Exe valley, almost at river level. At Feniton, beside the railway, the housing estate and fields named Burlands record the existence of another lowland group of barrows. The custom of barrow burial seems to have died out before 1,000 B.C.

Although barrows are numerous, the sites of Bronze-Age houses and settlements, except on Dartmoor, are elusive. Dartmoor has an immense concentration of hut circles and other Bronze-Age structures, but it is highly unlikely that similar settlements did not once occur all over Devon. A few sites have been discovered in Devon and Cornwall; one preserved under blown sand at Gwithian, where the furrows of a Bronze-Age plough and the digging marks of a Bronze-Age shovel have been revealed. The blade of the shovel matches that of the familiar long-handled Devon shovel, still in use today.

The extensive remains on Dartmoor survive probably because, since the climate deteriorated at the end of the Bronze Age and the peat started to build up, the moor has hardly ever been ploughed. The concentration of settlements on the southern moor is so thick that the population could not have been supported by, or engaged in, pastoral and arable farming alone. It seems that the people of the southern moor were working the tin deposits so necessary for the making of bronze, but virtually no archaeological evidence has been found to prove this theory.

10   An early Christian memorial stone at Ivybridge.

It may be that the deposits of tin have been worked over so frequently in historic times that all traces of ancient working have disappeared.

That the Bronze-Age population of the moor was considerable seems to have been conclusively demonstrated by the recent explanation of the widespread moorland 'reave' systems. Reaves are long low banks running often in parallel lines, across river valleys and over hill-tops. They divide the valleys of upper Dartmoor into long rectangles, often themselves sub-divided rather less regularly. Other reaves run along the watersheds between valleys and divide one group of parallels from another, and other contour reaves cut off the ends of the parallel groups from the open moor. Amongst these reaves are contemporary huts and small enclosures, again forming no regular pattern. The explanation offered is that these land divisions were established by communities to apportion the available farmland equitably, and to distinguish one group's land from another. It is not clear how these parallel divisions were used; they are often strewn with granite boulders, which would hinder ploughing, and the banks of the enclosures, the reaves themselves, do not seem ever to have been much higher than they are now, and so would not be effective barriers to livestock. Close and constant herding of the cattle might be as good as a strong fence, and the arable land may have been hand-tilled in some way, rather than being ploughed. The reave patterns when seen on a map seem elaborate and complicated, and suggest great pressure on the available land and an economy which was more than merely for subsistence. This remarkable Bronze-Age landscape is more extensive and elaborate than any similiar site in Europe. Reaves have not been recognised elsewhere in Devon, and it is tempting to suggest that the tin attracted so many folk to Dartmoor, that the division of the land had to be made to cope with this intensive settlement. The absence of reaves, and indeed of comparable settlement on Exmoor, can be explained tentatively by the absence of tin.

That there was considerable wealth amongst Bronze-Age people is shown by the elaborate and expensive metalwork discovered in the south-west. Palstaves, rapiers, bracelets and rings have all been discovered, some in hoards, many made locally. Other metalwork, including some of Irish gold, was imported, and most recently a wreck off Salcombe has produced bronze rapiers and a sword, suggesting a possible trade route. Rapiers and arrowheads apart, there is little evidence of war from the Bronze Age. Only one fortified site from this period has been found in south-west England. This may have been a 'golden age' of peace and plenty.

In contrast, the Iron Age, beginning in the south-west about 600 B.C., is best known and recognised by its hill-forts. These must be the products of a warlike or at least a feuding society, and it is possible that the peace of the Bronze Age broke down to such a degree that fortified hill-top villages, each with its own territory and chieftain, became the normal pattern. There is no clear evidence of a conquest, and this change in society may have been prompted by a deterioration in the climate,

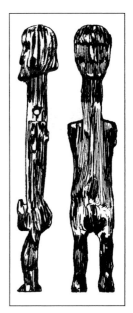

11 *Oak wooden idols, from Teigngrace, Newton Abbot.*

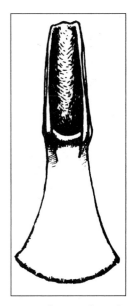

12 *Palstave of south-west type from Bovey Tracey.*

13 *Clovelly Dykes Iron-Age settlement, with pastoral enclosures for stock.*

14 *The Iron-Age settlement at Denbury, 'Devenebir' in 1228, the 'burh'—stronghold—of the men of Devon.*

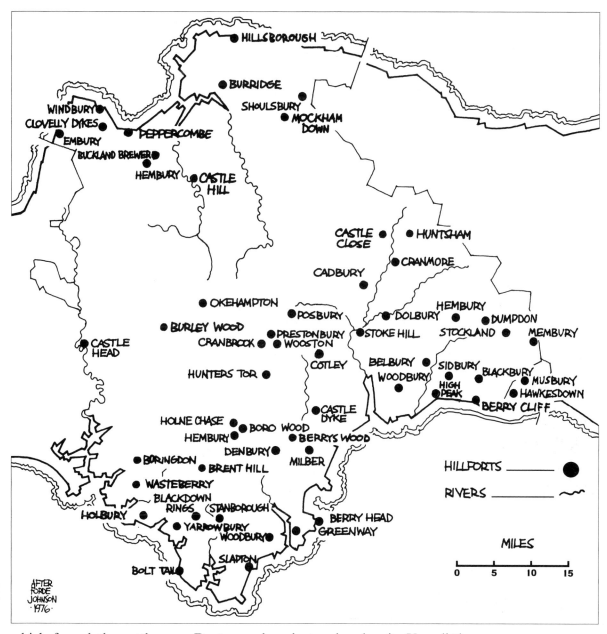

which forced the settlers on Dartmoor largely to abandon it. Very little   **15** *Iron-Age hill-forts.*
Iron-Age evidence has been found there.

There are some hundred Iron-Age hill-forts in Devon. They are of
various types. Some, like Embury near Hartland, and Bolt near Salcombe,
are cliff castles, similar to those built in Cornwall and Brittany. Some,
like Hembury and Sidbury, are large 'tribal' hill-forts, often occupying
the end of a spur and heavily fortified, either with single or more
dramatically multiple ditches. Most of the latter type are east of the Exe

*16 Decorated bronze
mirror.*

and may belong to the people of Dorset rather than Devon. A type peculiar to the south-west was found west of the Exe, with many enclosures within an all-embracing rampart, and a much smaller enclosure more or less in the centre. This may have contained the chieftain's hall and other houses, while the larger enclosures were for men and cattle, perhaps in times of danger. Small settlements known as 'rounds', with a single rampart, are numerous in Cornwall, and more have recently been recognised in Devon. These were perhaps family settlements, homesteads with simple defences. In Cornwall they were occupied into the Saxon period. Their relative absence in Devon may, once more, be because they have been destroyed, or lie under the floors of present-day farmhouses.

These Iron-Age folk are identifiable historically as the Dumnonii. To the Romans they were a recognisable tribe, although if they had a tribal capital it is unknown. No names of their tribal chieftains survive from this date, unlike those of some other tribes. They were, perhaps, already distinguishable from their western neighbours, the Cornovii of Cornwall, the 'people of the Horn' as opposed to the Dumnonii, the 'people of the Land', or perhaps as recently suggested, the 'worshippers of Dumnos'. The Dumnonii issued no coins, unlike their tribal neighbours to the east, but they traded with the Durotriges of Dorset, probably in cattle and minerals, though once again Dartmoor provides no evidence of mining activity.

The Dumnonii were not without sophistication. One of the most beautiful and elaborate objects to be excavated in recent years was found at Holcombe near Uplyme. It was a bronze mirror, elaborately engraved, dating from the first century A.D. In all, seven of these south-western mirrors are known and similar bronze collars and bowls have also been found, one bowl from as far away as Poland. Another one was found at Rose Ash in a bog. Evidence of Dumnonian resistance to the Romans is mounting, but their numerous hill-forts suggest that they lacked unity and cohesion, and were in fact still an amalgam of separate groups, each with its own local name and habitation. The old interpretation of their name is so indefinite as to add weight to this suggestion.

3

A Roman Backwater

Cornwall and Devon, and that part of Somerset west of the river Parrett, made up what was known to the Romans as Dumnonia. It cannot have been entirely unfamiliar to them before their invasion of Britain in A.D. 43. Its deposits of tin had been known about in the Mediterranean since the fourth century B.C., and there were trading links through France. Cornish tin was certainly being exported to Marseilles in the second century B.C. Caesar's expeditions in 55 and 54 B.C. brought him nowhere near Dumnonia, though it is likely that the Dumnonian tribes had supported the formidable Veneti of Armorica (Brittany) in their revolt against him in 56 B.C.

Rather more than a century later in A.D. 55, twelve years or so after their invasion of Britain in A.D. 43, the Second Roman Legion was in Exeter and the Roman presence is clearly recognisable in more than a score of sites in the South-West all dating from the first century A.D. when the occupation of Britannia was being consolidated. The hill-forts of the Dumnonii, their tribal centres, were probably abandoned, except where, as at Hembury, the Romans occupied the site briefly. The homesteads and farms of the native Dumnonii subdued by the Romans are not much in evidence, though increasing numbers have been recognised from aerial photographs.

At Exeter the Romans first built a fort of 36 acres barely large enough to hold the legion. From Exeter a road was pushed westward through Colebrooke, where there was a fort, to North Tawton where a fort and a camp and extensive enclosures have been photographed. This was probably *Nemetostatio*, named as a settlement in a Roman route book. It may take the first element of its name from the Celtic place-name element 'nymet'—meaning a sanctuary—still to be found in the locality in Nymet Rowland and Broad and Nicholls Nymet and Nymet Bridge. The original lines of this road from Exeter to North Tawton can be seen here and there in the lines of the hedgebanks. The outline of just such a sanctuary—a 'henge' monument—has been located by aerial photography in the vicinity. Beyond this to the west there were forts at Okehampton and Broadbury and at Carvoda, immediately west of the Tamar in Cornwall. Twenty miles further on was a fort at Nanstallon on the Camel and Carvossa near the Fal estuary which may be another military site, thus extending the Roman presence into West Cornwall.

17 *Inscriptions of the Dumnonii from Hadrian's Wall.*

27

18 Appledore and the estuary of the Taw and Torridge, the only 'deep' water access to the sea in North Devon, tidal and difficult. The covered shipbuilding yard in the bottom left-hand corner is the only working one in the South West.

To the north of the Dumnonian peninsula there is evidence of military activity near the mouths of the Taw and the Torridge. A temporary marching camp for brief occupation was built at Alverdiscott between Bideford and Barnstaple and close by there may be a more permanent fort at Newton Tracey. On the north coast there were two signal stations at Martinhoe and Countisbury, also dating from the first century, the latter being slightly earlier. They are sited so that their garrisons could observe activities in the Bristol Channel and along the coast of South Wales, where, at least until the '60s, the Silures were a considerable threat to Roman authority. Until his capture in A.D. 51, the Silures were led by Caractacus, a chieftain of more than merely tribal status.

Why the two coastal sites, together or in succession, were needed is not clear. Using beacon fires the garrisons could communicate with the Roman fleet which was perhaps based at Sea Mills near Avonmouth. Between North Devon and Exeter the only site so far known is a fort at Bury Barton near Lapford. To the east of the Taw valley lay some inhospitable country—the '*mor coed*', morchard or 'great wood' of Morchard Bishop and Cruwys Morchard.

To the west of the Exe there is another Roman military site near Exeter at Ide and in East Devon a number of others have been found. Within the great Iron-Age ramparts at Hembury was a Roman military post with buildings and a site for smelting the local deposits of iron found on the Blackdown Hills. These were worked both in Roman times and the Middle Ages. Woodbury near Axminster, close to where the Fosse Way and the Exeter to Dorchester road cross, has been shown to have survived as a considerable Roman settlement after its original military function ended. It may be that this was the so far unidentified *Moridunum*, recorded in a Roman route book of much later date, but another candidate for this 'lost' settlement is a recently discovered site beside the present A30 near Fenny Bridges, which would fit the recorded Roman mileages from Dorchester and Exeter far better than Woodbury.

In the valley of the Exe and its tributaries fortified sites have been identified at Tiverton, at Cullompton and at Killerton all overlooking likely trackways and routes, in particular the line of the present motorway/A38, surely always a way into the South West.

The main Roman route to Exeter branched off the Fosse Way—that great Roman highway from Lincoln to Axmouth via Leicester,

Cirencester, Bath and Ilchester—at Over Stratton just west of Ilchester. The route from there to Honiton is not clear. At Honiton it was joined by a road from Dorchester and Axminster. Here when the new Axminster by-pass was constructed the stone foundations of the old Roman road were clearly revealed following the most direct route across the Axe Valley as the by-pass does now. The line of the western end of this road from Honiton to Exeter can be most clearly seen where it passes Fairmile and Straitway Head and Strete Raleigh. These Saxon 'street' names suggest that to the Saxons this was a 'street', a paved road, and not an unpaved 'path' or a 'way'. However, when the M5 to Exeter was built no signs of stone Roman foundations like those at Axminster were found, surprisingly, where the line of the Roman road was crossed.

The Roman route books, already referred to, show that there was a recognised route down the south-western peninsula in Roman times— five Roman milestones have been found in Cornwall—from Dorchester to *Moridunum* 36 miles, to *Isca* another 15 miles and from thence to

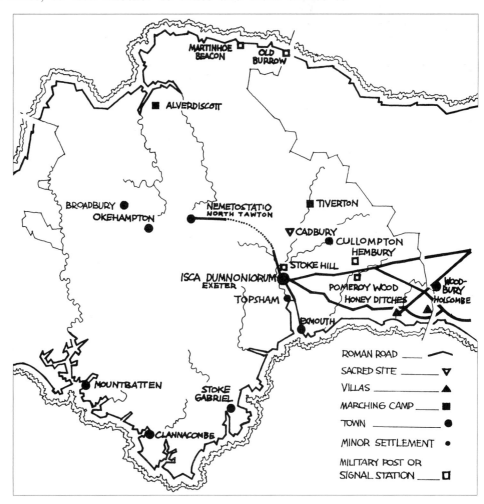

19 *Roman Devon.*

20 *A Roman signal station (first century A.D.) overlooking the Bristol Channel: Old Barrow, Countisbury.*

Nemetostatio and then to the unidentified *Devionissum statio* and *Tamaris* and *Uxella*. These roads and the sites associated with them were built and occupied as a consequence of the activities of the 2nd Legion under its legate Vespasian, in its conquest and occupation of the South West. They suggest some years of conflict, conquest and suppression; Vespasian is said to have 'fought thirty battles', 'reduced twenty strongholds' and 'subdued two tribes'.

The score or so of first-century military sites are barely matched, except at Exeter, by civil and domestic sites. At Holcombe near Lyme Regis there was a 'Villa' a 'country house' and there are perhaps traces of others at Membury, Whitestaunton, Combe St Nicholas and at Seaton, all at the eastern edge of the province of Dumnonia. Another villa fragment has been found at Budleigh Salterton, fairly recently and one has been identified near Crediton, but these five or six bear no comparison with the numerous and sometimes magnificent constructions found in the rest of lowland Roman Britain.

There are, however, remains of native sites of the Roman period to be found at Clannacombe near Thurlestone, at Stoke Gabriel on the Dart; there was a considerable trading settlement at Mountbatten near Plymouth, and a religious site at Cadbury in the Exe valley where votive offerings were found. A site may await discovery at Oldaport near Modbury on the Erme. Increasing numbers of Romano-British homesteads known as rounds have been recognised in Devon but there is not much to show where the native inhabitants of Devon lived during the three-and-a-half centuries of the Roman presence. Coins are widespread but are no indication of settlement, only of trade. A fine bronze figure of Cheiron and Achilles found at Sidmouth must once have adorned a villa or a temple though none is known nearby.

Exeter, *Isca Dumnoniorum*, was in contrast a considerable town in Roman times. The Second Augustan Legion was established there 12 years after the legions landed. The first Roman fort that was fortified with a palisade and bank was extended into something much larger; a full Roman city of 92 acres contained within the bounds of the present walls, whose foundations and lower courses are certainly Roman.

The legionary fort was developed with some sophistication. Outside the fort itself were civil settlements, a great bath house was built within what is now the cathedral close and behind the present Guildhall were barracks and legionary workshops. There were officers' houses in what is now South Street. The bath house was of some magnificence using high-quality imported stone for panelling and with the usual hypocaust and hot room. A naval port with granaries and store houses to supply the legion may have existed at Topsham.

By A.D. 75 the Romans were confident enough of their hold on Dumnonia to move the Second Legion to Caerleon in south Wales. It was needed there to assist in the subjugation of Wales and never returned

21 *Map of Roman Exeter.*

to Exeter, though it is possible that some sort of garrison was retained in the city. The Dumnonii made no known move at the time of Boudicca's rebellion in A.D. 60 though their attitude may have been threatening. The Second Legion was ordered to assist in the suppression of the rebellion but Postumus, the officer in charge at the time, refused to lead his men from Exeter, perhaps alarmed at what might occur in the legion's absence. Later he killed himself out of remorse at having denied his men a chance of military glory. This is the only human tale to emerge from the whole history of Roman Dumnonia.

By A.D. 80 the city, having lost its military function, became the capital of the Dumnonian people as *Isca Dumnoniorum*. It was to fulfil this function for the next three centuries. The Romans applied a form of indirect rule, similar to that employed later in the British empire, to their subject tribal territories. Leading men, chieftains of the Dumnonii, would have become members of the Council of the Civitas, responsible for tax collecting, recruitment and in part for law and order.

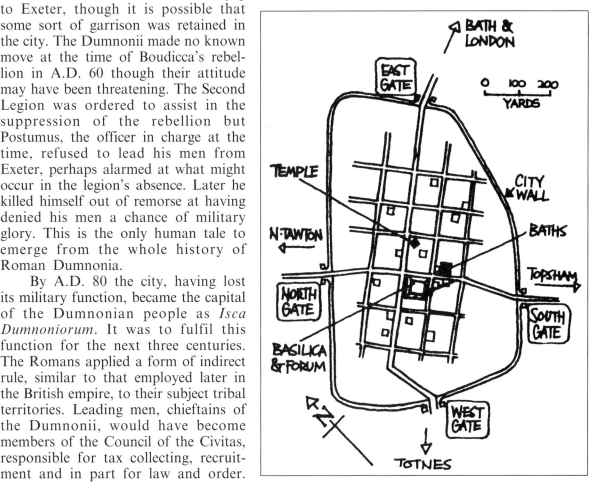

22 *Chi-Rho monogram on potsherd, Exeter.*

Tribal life and tribal laws and customs would perhaps have been allowed to continue under the rather distant eye of the Roman governor. This arrangement was cheap and least likely to cause trouble. To this end in Exeter the bath building was converted to a basilica, containing municipal offices; a new bath house was built and an open public forum or market place laid out. Eventually by A.D. 200 the city walls were fully constructed to enclose the city. The walls built out of local volcanic stone survive to this day as do the sites of the four city gates.

Exeter was quite a considerable city by contemporary standards. The houses were stone built, trade with the Mediterranean and Gaul flourished and a 'civilised' life was possible for the better off inhabitants. Outside the city Roman life and civilisation seems to have had little impact, judging by the apparent scarcity of villas, country houses and estates so far discovered within the boundaries of Dumnonia. East of the Exe and in the South Hams and Torbay, suitable fertile well-watered sites abound with as yet little trace of a 'civilised' Roman presence.

In A.D. 410 the Roman legions left Britain and the inhabitants were forced to fend for themselves. There is very little to say about the history of Devon in the three centuries between the arrival of the legion and its departure. By A.D. 380 the Roman forum was neglected and rubbish pits were dug into its surface. The Roman city was dying before the legions left, though it was probably never totally abandoned. A hoard of late Roman coins, buried and never recovered, found at Awliscombe near Honiton may be an indication of civil breakdown. The arrival of Christianity may be the most significant event of the last Roman century in Exeter and it is attested by a fragment of rough pottery with the *Chi Rho* Christian symbol scratched on it. In the next century it seems that the Dumnonian upper classes were Christian. These people reoccupied some of the hill-forts in what were troubled times and it may be that tribal life reasserted itself.

It is difficult to determine the influence of those three centuries of Roman rule. The Dumnonian chiefs and princes surely became rather less than they were, if, as seems likely, their hill-forts, their courts and castles were abandoned. For the lesser folk it is probably quite wrong to distinguish between Roman and Briton after a time. They were all citizens of the Empire and some would have been, like St Paul, full Roman citizens. All free men had that status by the early third century. But life in *Isca*, civilised town life, would have been different from the life of the Dumnonian peasant and there was no *Isca* before or for many years after the Romans. Outside the towns native life probably changed little. Apart from Cornish tin—and there is no firm evidence of Roman tin mining on Dartmoor—and Blackdown iron, there was little to attract the pressing attention of the Imperial Government. *Isca* apart, Dumnonia seems to have been something of a Roman backwater.

I *Merivale Stone Row. One of some seventy ritual or boundary rows on Dartmoor, from the Bronze Age. This is 46 yds long; a row on Stall Moor measures 2½ miles, the longest in the world.*

II *Spinster's Rock. A shilstone or shelf stone, a burial chamber from the New Stone Age, one of four surviving and six destroyed in Devon. The name suggests some lost folk attribute or use.*

III *Beardown Man. A menhir standing by itself. From the Bronze Age, sometimes associated with burials. Man is probably just 'maen' a stone, in the old Celtic language, but this stone is startlingly upright and manlike. The tallest menhir known in Cornwall was 24ft high.*

IV *Okehampton Castle. Begun just after the Norman Conquest on the main road from Exeter to Cornwall by Baldwin the Sherriff of Devon, the ancestor of the Earls of Devon. The only Devon castle mentioned in Domesday Book.*

4

The Men of Defenascire

In the year 614 the kings Cynegils and Cwichelm fought at 'Beandun' and 'slew two thousand and sixty-five Britons'. This battle, almost certainly at Bindon near Axmouth, marks the beginning of the Saxon conquest of Dumnonia. In the two centuries between that date and the end of Roman rule, traditionally in 410, little is known of Dumnonian history. A few shadowy names emerge from the darkness: Geraint, who was slain at 'Longborth' about 480, a 'hero of the land of Dyfnaint'; Cato, who was king of Dumnonia under the overlordship of Arthur, perhaps in about 500; and the evil Constantine, 'the unclean whelp of the lioness of Dumnonia'. Arthur himself, a genuinely historical figure, has no traditional associations with Devon although plenty with Cornwall. He was the 'supreme commander who defeated the English', and the Dumnonian kings and princes were almost certainly his allies.

With the end of Roman rule the old Celtic life reasserted itself. Petty kings and tyrants like Constantine, denounced by Gildas the scribe, emerged and claimed their ancestors' lost authority. Many Britons fled across the Channel to Brittany to escape these troubles, and founded the kingdoms of Domnonie and Cornuaille. Brittany, once Armorica, became truly the 'land of the Britons'. The roots of the Breton language are Dumnonian.

Christianity survived and persisted. The Christian memorial stones found in Cornwall, south Wales, and in Devon on the western borders and on Exmoor, indicate this clearly. Some have ancient Irish 'ogam' inscriptions. From Ireland and south Wales came missionary 'saints' to preach the faith in the South-West. Celtic 'monasteries' certainly preceded some medieval abbeys in Devon, and some present-day parish churches may also occupy Celtic sites. There was a flowering of Celtic civilisation and culture around the shores of the Irish Sea and the Western Channel, while further east the rest of England was in the hands of the still pagan Saxon kingdoms.

By 577, the Saxons, having been checked in their advance for half a century or so by Arthur, and the fragile unity that followed him, resumed their attacks on Dumnonia. In that year, having fought at Dyrham near Bath on the edge of the Cotswolds, they reached the Severn, thus dividing those they called the Welsh in south Wales from the West

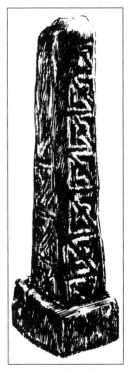

23 *Saxon cross shaft, St Nicholas's Priory, Exeter.*

33

24 *St Winwaloe.*

Welsh in Dumnonia. A generation or so later, they were on the borders of Devon at Bindon.

However, it was not to be for another hundred years or so—three or four generations—that the Saxons reached the banks of the Tamar. In 710 King Ine of Wessex fought against another Geraint of Dumnonia, and a year later he granted Glastonbury Abbey large estates in Cornwall, just across the Tamar on the Lynher river. Certainly, by 720 the Saxons were fighting well into Cornwall, probably on the Camel estuary, near Padstow.

Devon was therefore the last part of Britain which the Saxons conquered and absorbed. The Saxon settlement stopped at the River Tamar roughly, although there are Saxon place-names in east Cornwall. The time-scale of the Saxon occupation, a century or so from the Axe to the Tamar—70 miles by road—implies no massive conquering armies that swept Devon from end to end. It seems to have been some fifty years after Bindon before the Saxons reached Exeter. In 661 they were fighting at Posentesburh, perhaps Posbury near Crediton, and by 682 they had driven the Dumnonian Welsh 'as far as the sea', perhaps to the south of Hartland. The Saxon St Boniface was at school in Exeter by at least 680.

This slow advance may have been due to the West Saxons' need in the seventh century to defend themselves against the all-powerful Mercian kingdom to the north of them, but it is also likely that Saxon penetration was initially peaceful; landless Saxon peasants, younger sons, pushing westwards into the hills of what may have been a thinly-populated Devon. Eventually a local clash between Saxon and Briton might escalate into a full-scale war, with armies led by the West Saxon kings and battles noted in the chronicles. The Saxons were perhaps less sophisticated and civilised than the Britons they conquered.

In the South-West, the Dumnonian Welsh, disunited, cut off by land from their kinsmen in Wales, were unable to resist Saxon pressure. They were not exterminated or driven overseas *en masse*, though some may have taken refuge with their cousins in Brittany. The laws of the Saxon King Ine made careful provision for cases involving the surviving Welsh, even if compensation for the death of a Welshman was less than for that of a Saxon. They were a subject race, but they were still part of the community. In Devon no Welshmen of importance are known.

In Devon, almost all the place-names are Saxon; a greater proportion than in, for instance, Dorset. But there are groups of seemingly Welsh names, or names with Welsh elements, that may show that the Welsh survived in some numbers. Aunk and Whimple in east Devon, Molland, Bray and Charles on the borders of Exmoor, Dunchideock and Trusham on Haldon Hill are all Celtic names, at least in part. In the South Hams, between Dartmouth and Plymouth, there are Penquit, Crowdy, Coarsewell, Clickland, Keaton, Cornworthy, Cornwood, all farm or village names, all again, in part at least, Celtic. At Portlemouth, near Salcombe, the name itself may be partly Celtic; the church has a Celtic dedication (to St Winwaloe); and nearby is Walland, which, like Wallaton in East Allington and Walreddon near Tavistock, refers probably to a group of the Welsh. Close by is Kernborough, which like Portlemouth is a hybrid word, partly Celtic and partly Saxon, both parts meaning much the same in either language, and used perhaps by Welsh and Saxon contemporaneously. In Saxon times the road from Kingsbridge to Totnes was referred to as 'the Welsh way'.

Perhaps the best evidence of British survival is provided by the shrewd piece of detective work done by Professor Finberg on two Anglo-Saxon charters which refer to Treable in Cheriton Bishop. In 739 a large land-grant was made by King Ethelheard of Wessex to the church of Crediton. The boundaries of the land so granted make a quite illogical detour to avoid the Treable area, so that it did not become Crediton's property. Nearly two and a half centuries later, King Edward the Elder made a grant of 'Hyples old land' to one of his thegns, Aelfsige. The land granted corresponds, in Prof. Finberg's view, almost exactly with that illogically omitted from the Crediton Charter. It seems likely that it was not granted to Crediton because it belonged to someone too important to offend. His name, or his descendant's or successor's name, may have been Hyple; 'Treable' is in fact the 'trev' (farm) of Hyple or Ebel. The name is entirely Celtic. By 976, however, it had become possible to absorb this Celtic enclave. Perhaps this was because, as William of Malmesbury says, King Aethelstan had driven the Britons from Exeter, 'cleansed the city of that filthy race', and made the Tamar the boundary between Celt and Saxon. Evidently two centuries of co-existence between Celt and Saxon in Devon had ended in acrimony, and a transference of the Welsh population across the Tamar had become desirable. By that time, however, much intermarriage must have taken place, and Devon's native population must contain much Celtic blood. No wonder that Aethelstan features largely in Cornish folktale.

The Welsh may have survived in some numbers, but it remains true that the overwhelming majority of Devon place-names are Saxon, whether towns, villages or isolated farms. The Saxon takeover seems to have been pretty complete. But the types of place-name are not uniform. Names ending in '-ing' or '-ings', indicating in some forms a folk or a people, are absent from Devon. Names ending in '-ingtun', meaning 'a village founded by a prominent individual and his dependents', number about forty in the county. Other suffixes, indicating where people lived, are '-ton', '-cot', '-worthy', and '-hayes', although this latter strictly means 'hedges', i.e. a hedged enclosure. 'Hayes' is common east of the Exe, up to and across the Dorset border. 'Cot' is common in north Devon and west Somerset, but largely absent in east and south Devon. 'Worth' or 'worthy' has the same distribution as 'cot', but there are a few exceptions in east and south Devon. 'Ton' is widely distributed, but is most common where 'cot' and 'worthy' are absent: in east Devon it is rare. If 'cot' and 'worthy' mean, as has been suggested, the 'cottage of a poor peasant' and 'the home of a substantial freeman' respectively, then the Saxon settlement of north Devon was of a rather different nature in comparison with the

25 *Inscribed sword guard made of bronze, Exeter: 'Leofric made me'.*

areas where '-ton', a village, a 'collection of houses', and '-ington' predominate. The north of the county may have been less attractive: clayey, wet, windy, heavily wooded. The south perhaps attracted earlier settlers, while north Devon was conquered later. King Ine built a fort at Taunton, but this was demolished mysteriously by his queen in 722, perhaps because north Devon and west Somerset were still debatable country. However, by 1086 when Domesday Book was compiled, north Devon was well settled, and its place-names predominantly Saxon.

In the ninth century, conflict with the surviving Welsh in Cornwall persisted. In 815, King Egbert of Wessex 'harried Cornwall from east to west', but this did not prevent a Cornish raid into Devon at Galford near Lifton in 825. In 838 the Cornish allied with a Viking army against the Saxons, but were defeated by Egbert at Hingston Down, just across the Tamar from Tavistock. That is the last that is known of Cornish resistance.

Devon suffered extensively from later Viking raids. In 851 Ceorl, an ealdorman of Devon, defeated the Danes at 'Wicganbeorgh', perhaps Weekaborough in Torbay. In 876 another ealdorman, Odda, fought off 23 shiploads of Vikings at Countisbury. Odda and 800 others were killed, however. In that year the Danish army wintered in Exeter. A century or so later, Devon suffered again. Between 990 and 1003, the Danes sacked Tavistock and King's Teignton and besieged Exeter, burning Pinhoe and Broadclyst. Exeter was betrayed to them in 1003, and they sacked the city. Doubtless many coastal villages also suffered. More peacefully, the Danish king Cnut founded Buckfast Abbey in 1018. The Danes did not settle in Devon as they did in eastern England. Lundy has a Viking name, as has the Skerries Bank off the Start. Grimstone, Oldstone, Farmstone, Gripstone and Dorsely in the South Hams have possible Scandinavian prefixes in their names. But that is all.

Little is known of the internal history of Devon during the Saxon centuries. The county was at some date divided into 33 hundreds for administrative purposes, so that taxes might be collected, law and order enforced and armies raised. The boundaries of these hundreds, as they are known from Domesday Book, seem to reflect more the administrative convenience of local landowners than any logical geographical division of the county. Wonford hundred, in which Exeter lay, stretched out nearly as far as Okehampton, and included ten hides of land to the west of the Teign, in which lay Stoke and Combe in Teignhead. These were, and should now be, more properly, Stoke and Combe in the Ten Hides. Haytor hundred included much of Torbay with a detached portion around Haytor itself. Nine of Devon's hundreds had detached outliers, sometimes many miles away.

To establish some sort of defensive system against the Danes, King Alfred designated four 'burhs' or strongholds in Devon, and many others in other counties. Halwell on the high ground between Totnes and Kingsbridge, Pilton above Barnstaple, Lydford and Exeter were the chosen strong-points. With the Danish threat gone, defence was no longer so vital, and Halwell and Pilton gave way to Totnes and Barnstaple.

26 *Saxon-style windows of Exeter Castle gatehouse.*

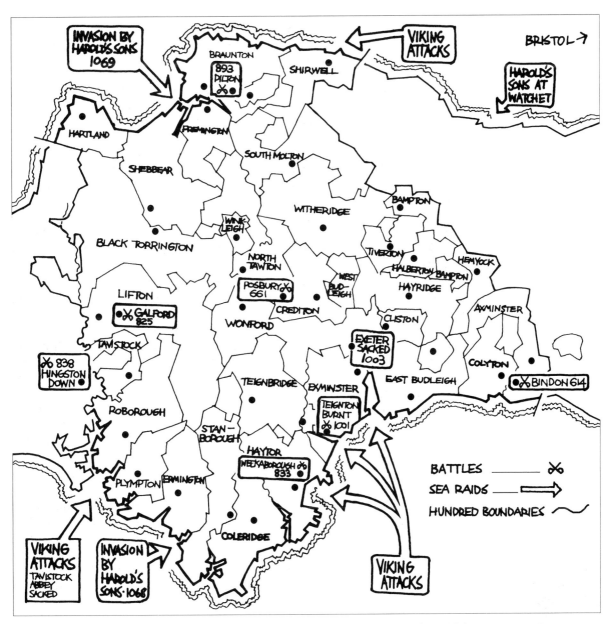

27 *Battles and sea raids in Saxon Devon.*

These, with Exeter and Lydford, were the four towns of Devon by 1086, with their own burgesses, markets and mints, and perhaps churches, castles and walls as well.

The lower valley of the Axe was clearly of some importance in Saxon times. It may be that the Axe was navigable, and Axmouth a port in those days. King Edward the Elder held a 'Witan' or Saxon royal council at Axminster in 901, and King Edmund's council of 945 met at Colyton. Both places had 'minster' churches with considerable estates in 1066, and Axminster must have had a church or burial ground as early as 786, when the West Saxon prince Cyneheard was buried there. At Colyton one of the few Saxon crosses in Devon survives, and at both places there must have been buildings (perhaps belonging to the church) of sufficient size to house the king, his court, the bishops and noblemen and their servants. Both places were also hundredal centres. Axminster had dependent estates at Honiton, Membury and elsewhere, and Colyton church owned St Olaf's church and other property in Exeter. Axminster was royal in 1086 and King Alfred the Great had owned both Axmouth and Branscombe personally. They, along with Cullompton, Exminster, Whitchurch, Lifton, Hartland, Lustleigh and Tiverton figure in his will. At five of these seven places there were probably churches. Edward the Elder held a council in Exeter in 920 and Athelstan's Witans were at Exeter in 928 and 935 and at Lifton in 931.

28 *The Saxon 'copelan stan' at Copplestone, where three parishes meet, mentioned in a charter of 974.*

Some 70 Saxon charters or 'landbooks' exist for Devon. These mostly record grants of land by 'book'. The land so granted became 'bookland', frequently corrupted to 'buckland', which could then be granted by the owner at will, and not inherited automatically by his kinsfolk. Many were grants to the church. A number of these record the boundaries of

the estates granted, in Anglo-Saxon. Some of the places mentioned are still readily identifiable, but many refer to streams, hills, dikes, cliffs, thorn trees, barrows and earthworks whose names are long forgotten. One notable survival is the 'Copelastone' at Copplestone, where three parishes meet, recorded in a charter of 974. The charters range in date from 729 to 1066, and the size of land granted from virtually the whole eastern half of the South Hams to thirty acres or so at Kenton. About half are grants of land in the perhaps more settled districts around Crediton and to the east of the Exe. Doubtless many more charters have perished.

Parallel to the hundredal organisation there must have been some sort of ecclesiastical system as well. When Bindon was fought in 614, Augustine's mission to the Saxons from Rome was 17 years old, and Augustine himself had been dead for ten. Cynegils, who fought at Bindon, was baptised *c.*635, so it is likely that the Saxons were, if not Christian, aware of and influenced by Christianity when they were conquering Devon. By 680 there was a Saxon

29 *Swete's drawing of East Teignmouth old church, now destroyed, mentioned in a charter of 1044. Swete was convinced it was a Saxon building.*

church and school in Exeter. No pagan Saxon remains have ever been found in Devon.

As they moved west, the Saxons must have come more and more into contact with folk who were already Christian. It may be, in fact, that Devon, like Wales and Cornwall, but unlike the lands further east, never ceased to be Christian in some fashion, since Christianity first came to these islands.

The first organisation of the Saxon church seems to have been based on the 'minster', a large church with a priestly or monastic resident community, intended to serve a considerable neighbourhood. This arrangement was not unlike the Celtic monastery, which functioned apparently in much the same way. Exminster and Axminster are obvious examples, but others can be identified at Colyton, Cullompton, Plympton, Kingskerswell, St Marychurch, Yealmpton, South Molton and Woodbury. Others, which may derive from the Celtic tradition, were at Braunton, Hartland (Stoke St Nectan), Hollacombe near Holsworthy, Newton St Petrock, Bridestowe, Marystowe, and perhaps Lifton. 'Stow' as a suffix implies a holy place in the Saxon language. Christow, Instow (St John's Stow), Churchstow, Virginstow, may all have been minster or early sites of churches, before each individual parish acquired a church. Some 40 places can be identified as having churches, priests or some religious association by 1086. The only surviving Saxon church architecture in Devon is the 'crypt' at Sidbury, though the old church at Teignmouth, recorded before 1066, may have been Saxon.

Crediton was the seat of the first bishop in Devon. Church matters had been administered from Sherborne until the early tenth century. St Germans became the seat of the Cornish bishop at the same time, but in 1050 the two bishoprics were amalgamated and the see transferred to Exeter.

Ecclesiastically and politically, therefore, Devon was a recognisable entity well before the Norman Conquest, since in 851 the Anglo-Saxon Chronicle refers to 'the men of Defenascire'. The present boundaries of

30 *Anglo-Saxon cross shaft, Colyton parish church.*

31   *Saxon Devon and its religious sites.*

Devon, with a few minor exceptions, were drawn in Saxon times. It is in fact from this period that the history of the county proper can be said to begin. Whether the landscape of Devon is a Saxon one is very much less clear. It seems likely that the farms and village sites of Devon are pre-Saxon, however. Apart from the hill-forts, abandoned in Roman times and not certainly re-occupied thereafter, the Bronze-Age remains on Dartmoor, and the Roman forts and villas, there are few pre-Saxon habitation sites recorded in the county. Yet it was not sparsely populated, as the Saxon campaigns demonstrate. The conclusion must be that the old sites were taken over by the Saxon conquerors and renamed. Much of the present-day hedged and enclosed landscape may be the work of Saxon peasants, but created over a long period as the population expanded. What was there before them is quite unknown, but present research would not suggest, even in upland Devon, that a total wilderness awaited the Saxon axe and plough.

5

Norman Devon

In the year 1068 William the Conqueror came to Exeter. The city had risen in rebellion, shut its gate and refused to acknowledge the Norman king. It had allied itself with other western towns and encouraged them to rebel. William took hostages from a delegation of citizens but, when he arrived, he found the gates closed. He promptly had a hostage blinded. One nameless but audacious Exeter man responded 'out of contempt of the Normans ... having bared himself, standing on the walls, [he] disturbed the ears with a sound from his lower parts'. The king could do nothing for 18 days. Exeter eventually received him, swore loyalty and in return suffered no sack or damage. It is not recorded what happened to that daring Exonian who had insulted him.

However, this was not the last trouble for the Normans in Devon. The order of events is unclear, but in the years 1068 and 1069 there were at least four other attempts to defy and eject the Normans. Harold Godwinson—King Harold of England—had had at least three grown sons living when he was killed at Hastings. They had taken refuge with King Diarmid of Dublin, ruler of a Viking settlement. From there they raided Bristol in 1068, but were repulsed and then landed in north Somerset where they fought a drawn battle with the Saxon ealdorman of Somerset, Eadnoth the Staller, now loyal to the new ruler. Eadnoth was killed and Harold's sons took ship again. Either in the same year or the following one, they landed at the mouth of the Taw and the Torridge, where they were repulsed probably by Baldwin de Brionne, the Norman sheriff of Devon.

In 1069 they came again to the South Hams and laid waste nine manors near Thurlestone. One version has it that they besieged Exeter once more. Certainly it seems that there was another siege of the city in 1069 and that this time the citizens were loyal to William, since they repulsed the besiegers and drove them off. At the same time, the castle or fort on Ham Hill at Montacute was besieged by rebels, and was relieved by the Norman bishop of Coutances, a considerable tenant-in-chief of the king in Devon. Eventually the rebels were put to flight and there was seemingly no more trouble in the west. It may be that the focus of all this activity was Harold's family, the Godwinsons, who had between them considerable possessions in the west. Harold himself had owned Topsham and 15 other manors in Devon. This may be why Harold's sons

32 *Totnes Castle.*

33 *Axminster Church, the Norman door. There has been a 'minster' church here since the eighth century, when the Prince or Atheling Cyneheard, of the royal house of Wessex, was slain in a feud and buried 'at Axminster'.*

chose the county as the setting for two of their rebellions against William, perhaps counting on a local rising to support them. It may also be that the rising in the west was only part of a planned attempt against William from all sides—there was a Danish fleet in the north in 1069—which was never properly coordinated.

Within the next couple of generations, at least twenty castles had been built by the Normans in Devon. There are still substantial remains at Plympton, Exeter, Totnes, Okehampton and Lydford, but the rest are largely earthworks, remains of mottes and baileys, some on Iron-Age sites. Blackdown near Loddiswell, and Heywood near Chulmleigh are obvious examples of these. In all there may be as many as 24 of these scattered over the county. Some of these mottes and baileys may date from the troubles of Stephen's reign, when for instance Bampton and Exeter and Plympton were all fought over. That there were so many may imply a real danger of rebellion against Norman rule. Ten are grouped in and around the upper valleys of the Taw and Torridge. These may have been built to protect the interior of Devon from raids such as that of Harold's sons. This may also be the explanation of Blackdown Rings overlooking the area around Thurlestone, also attacked in 1069, and indeed of other such sites. If this is so, then clearly these attacks were the cause of some alarm.

Whether Devon tended to be loyal to the Godwinsons or not, it is clear that by 1086, the date of the Domesday Survey, almost all the Saxon landowners had lost their lands. In Devon 23 Saxons still held directly of the king, owning 54 manors between them, out of the thousand or so manors recorded for the county in Domesday Book. One of them, Colvin, held eight manors, and another, Godwin, held ten. Colvin was a reeve, an official of some sort, and two other members of the group, Adret and Aluric, were foresters. These three possibly retained their land by virtue of their offices. For the rest, there is no explanation. Making allowances for alternative spellings of the same name, it is possible to distinguish some 147 Saxon landowners in 1066 in Devon. This is a minimum figure. By 1086, apart from the 23 Saxon thanes, there were only 50 tenants-in-chief. Amongst these must be included the church. The bishop of Exeter, the abbots of Tavistock, Buckfast, Glastonbury and Horton with others owned 52 manors which had been owned by their predecessors in 1066. The king himself was in possession of 24 large estates which had belonged to Edward the Confessor. Everything else in Devon had changed hands between 1066 and 1086.

Out of the 1,000 Domesday estates, some 130 only remained in the hands of those who had owned them at the Conquest. Nearly three-quarters of what was left was in the hands of only six men. These were Baldwin de Brionne, the sheriff; Judel of Totnes, probably a Breton; the bishop of Coutances, who held as a layman; Ralf de Pomeroy and his brother William Capra; and the king's half-brother, Robert, Count of Mortain. These six held some 560 manors between them. Count Robert of Mortain had enormous estates elsewhere in the country, so that power in Devon was doubtless wielded by the remaining five. No great block of land was granted to any one man, all their estates being widely scattered. Apart from that principle, it is impossible to guess how the distribution was worked out. The rest were divided among 37 lesser Norman tenants. Beneath these great tenants-in-chief were innumerable sub-tenants, some of whom themselves held many manors, like Reginald de Valletort, who gave his name to Sutton Vautort in Plymouth. What this great transfer of land, only matched in later centuries at the Dissolution of the Monasteries, meant to the Devonshire peasant tilling the soil, is unknown; probably very little.

A great many entries in Domesday Book tell of thanes who in 1066 held their land freely and 'could go to what lord they willed' but whose land was now absorbed in a superior manor. Up at Gappah on Haldon in 1066, five thanes lived, who could 'go to what lord they liked'. By 1086, Gappah was Ralf de Pomeroy's property. What happened to these men is unknown, but it is tempting to see in the two cottagers, whom the Count of Mortain had at Little Faringdon, the two brothers who had held the land freely in 1066. In 1086 there were still 120 estates whose ownership was in some way in dispute. They had been 'occupied' by Normans without the king's permission. In the aftermath of the Conquest the law could be ignored and might was right; Saxons resisted at their peril. It does not seem that Devonshire people acquiesced too readily. They had lost status and property and were, surely, less free than they had been before 1066.

In 1086 the king ordered that a detailed assessment be made of his kingdom for tax purposes. This is Domesday Book, which provides a useful foundation on which to build an account of Devon in the Middle Ages. It is primarily concerned with ownership and value, and not concerned with what was not taxable, and thus omits information which can only occasionally be supplied from other sources. The survey names 983 manors in Devon, most of which can still be identified. It lists four towns—Exeter, Barnstaple, Totnes and Lydford—and one place, Okehampton, where there were four 'townsmen'. For nearly all the 983

34 *Norman doorway, St Peter's Church, Tiverton.*

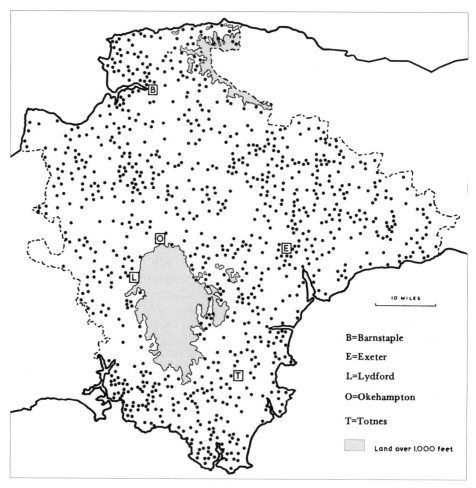

B=Barnstaple

E=Exeter

L=Lydford

O=Okehampton

T=Totnes

Land over 1,000 feet

10 MILES

manors it states the present (1086) and past (1066) owners, the number of 'villagers', 'smallholders' and 'slaves' resident there, the past and present value of the manor, and the amount of land, expressed in terms of ploughlands, or what one plough could cope with in a year.

In all Devon there were 8,519 villagers, 4,876 smallholders or lesser tenants, 3,323 slaves and 590 others, a total listed population of 17,308. Domesday Book then lists the livestock on the lord of the manor's own farm, his 'demesne', and the amount of woodland, meadow and rough pasture on each manor. It lists mills where they existed and shows that there were 'salterns' in 28 places in Devon, where salt water was boiled or evaporated to make salt, and 16 places had fisheries where salmon were netted or caught in a fishing weir. Churches were recorded at only nine places, though priests are mentioned at another seven. There were two abbeys—Buckfast and Tavistock—and two markets, at Okehampton and Otterton.

Domesday Book indicates further that both Dartmoor and Exmoor were upland grazing areas where stock from neighbouring manors was pastured in summer, as well as the ancestors of the present Dartmoor and Exmoor ponies. There were 370 swineherds—nearly three-quarters of the total number for England. There were four ironworkers in North Molton, five beekeepers, 61 saltworkers, two fishermen and two smiths. In 1086 slaves made up a higher proportion of the population of Devon than of any other south-western county apart from Cornwall. This might indicate the existence of an enslaved Celtic element. It is possible to make rough calculations of the total population of the county. A conventional figure of five per family would give a total population of 85,000, unless slaves are regarded as individuals and not as heads of families, in which case a figure of 73,000 is reached. Almost certainly there were other folk—freemen, churchmen, the lords of the manors themselves—who were not recorded at all.

The 983 places mentioned in Domesday Book were well distributed around the county, apart from the great uninhabited waste of Dartmoor. Those empty spaces that there are, for instance around Crediton, may perhaps be explained by the nature of the record. Crediton had 185 plough teams and 224 villagers, but it is highly unlikely that all those villagers lived where the town stands today—this entry probably conceals a number of farms and hamlets scattered over a large area.

It is likely that each of the 8,519 recorded villagers was a farmer with his own farm. Frequently, a manor with five villagers recorded in 1086 can be shown still to have had five farms three centuries later. There were probably some 10,000 farms in Devon in 1086. The impression given by Domesday Book is that of a countryside already well settled. This impression is strengthened by the fact that, at sites like Natsworthy on Dartmoor, there were farms at 1,200 feet, close to or above the height of any subsequent settlement. In 1086 Dartmoor apart, nowhere in Devon was without its farms, hamlets and villages. It seems likely that there was, nevertheless, still much waste land in Devon, when its tax value of 1,159 hides is compared with Somerset and Wiltshire, assessed at 2,902 and 3,893 hides respectively. But 695 of Devon's manors—71 per cent—did not have, it seems, enough ploughs to cultivate the available ploughlands. This may conceal an unrecorded population of freemen, with their own ploughs. However, a further possibility is that much land in Devon was tilled only occasionally. But it is clear that, despite its size and potential, the county was assessed to pay taxes at a low rate.

This suggestion of a rather backward economy is perhaps borne out by the relative absence of water mills. Only 83 places in Devon had them (eight per cent of the total) compared with 42 per cent in Somerset and 58 per cent in Wiltshire. In all there were 99 mills, and three-quarters of these were in or east of the Exe valley. This can only be explained by suggesting that the water mill was a new and expensive device that had in 1086 barely reached as far as the Exe valley. By 1500, in contrast, it is likely that every little stream turned its quota of tumbling overshot wheels. Economic backwardness in 1086 and economic growth in the medieval period could hardly be better illustrated.

36 *William the Conqueror's gate tower, Exeter Castle, with Saxon-style windows.*

6

Farms, Villages and Fields

Devon has a landscape made by peasants. The small fields and high banks are very largely the work of the men who farmed the land themselves. Here and there, around great houses, are the tailored parks and plantations of 18th-century gentlemen, and earlier there were deer parks; earlier still, great earthern Saxon boundary banks. But these apart, generation after generation of peasants have cleared the scrub, grubbed the roots, shifted the boulders, built the banks and ploughed the fields. It is a landscape of hard physical toil. The Devon banks, such a feature of the landscape, five to six feet high, turf-faced, topped with blackthorn, hazel or ash, must be the product of times when there were folk in plenty on the land. Well maintained, the hedges provide a good stock-proof fence, shelter from wind and rain, and regular firewood. They are most obvious and well-developed where surface stone is absent; only Dartmoor is really without them. They occupy a vast amount of land, and the toil to build and maintain them was enormous. They are not easily explicable, but clearly they always made good sense to their makers, since land enclosed from the common as late as the 19th century still has such banks as boundaries. The fields they enclose are mostly small, and their shapes are often haphazard. Only here and there, where there was 18th- and 19th-century enclosure of the common waste, can the surveyors' straight lines be seen. The intricate asymmetry of the rest is the result of agrarian arrangements and agreements made between peasant and peasant, and tenant and landlord.

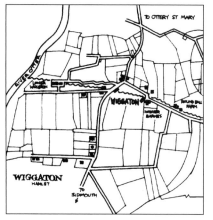

37 *Wiggaton: the hamlet of Wiggaton in the parish of Ottery St Mary. Wiggaton is 'Wicga's farm', perhaps to be linked with 'Wicgincland' referred to in a charter of 1061. A dozen or so houses had their own field system and strips.*

At first sight, the principal features are small irregular hedged fields, and isolated farms. This is in fact an inaccurate image. All over the county, but perhaps more frequently in the south, there are big agricultural villages, often at a meeting-place of roads, their streets lined with husbandmen's houses dating apparently from the 16th or 17th centuries. Such are Ugborough, Otterton, Broadhembury, Thorverton, Blackawton, Bradworthy, Sidbury and Braunton. Some, like Ottery St Mary and Colyton, grew eventually into market towns, centres of rural industry; some, like Silverton, Woodbury and Chillington, acquired 'borough' status in medieval times, with a charter, fair and 'burgesses'.

All of them had good populations in Domesday Book and a good many were royal property, 'ancient demesne'. None show any signs of means of defence other than their layout of roads and houses, but Woodbury, Broadhembury, Membury, Sidbury, Musbury and Denbury all nestle beneath hill-forts and take their names from them.

At one time these big villages were thought of as the primary settlements from which further colonisation developed. Alternatively, they were thought of as perhaps Saxon settlements in a Celtic landscape. Modern research has shown, however, that elsewhere in England big villages developed late in the history of the landscape, as the population grew and wealth increased. This may well apply to Devon villages, though this is quite uncertain.

At the opposite extreme to the big village is the isolated farm, perhaps the most characteristic feature of the Devon landscape. Often at the end of a lane, surrounded, seemingly haphazardly, by farm buildings, often a mile or more from a neighbour, with its lands and fields tidily within a ring fence, the Devonshire farm may have all sorts of origins. It may be the fruit of one family's struggle to carve out a viable holding from the waste, taking it in, field by field, year by year, from the wood or the moor. Its name may be—rarely—Celtic, or more commonly Saxon, describing some natural feature, a hill, ford, cliff or clearing, and combining that with the name of a previous owner, Saxon, medieval or modern. Many with names of recent origin must have had other older ones.

There may now be only one farm where there were once two or more, with their fields intermingled and worked in common. Some may be squatters' houses, built on the common, taking in the odd acre here and there with dubious legality. A few are enclosure farms, planted on

38 *Ugborough, a typical 'nucleated' village, with a central square, large church and farms. The South Hams landscape beyond.*

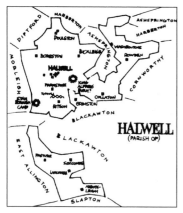

39 *Halwell: the old parish boundaries taken from the tithe survey, c.1840. A 'church town' settlement, 'the holy spring', with a small central settlement around the church and many scattered farms. The parish comprises what was left of a ridge of high moory land, probably once common to all the surrounding parishes before their boundaries became fixed. King Alfred established a burgh, a stronghold, here in the 10th century to counter the activities of the Danes. Stanborough, probably originally of Iron-Age date, later became a Saxon Hundred meeting place. Farmstone, Grimston and adjoining Gripstone, Oldstone and Dorsely (not shown) bear seemingly Scandinavian names.*

common land, enclosed and laid out by Act of Parliament during the last two centuries. Many more may derive, indirectly, from the enclosure of the medieval common fields, strip being joined to strip and the result being hedged and exchanged to make compact holdings, by the mutual consent of the villagers and the lord of the manor. This could be done most easily when, for instance, population declined and land was left unoccupied. Clearly, there is no one explanation of the isolated farm.

Between the two extremes of the large village and the single farmstead, there are other types of settlement. The most obvious is the hamlet, almost as characteristic of the Devon landscape as the isolated farm. This may be a group of two or more farms and a few cottages, once perhaps also separate farms. The hamlet may be close-set or scattered along a road, in a combe where there was a water supply, or with no obvious focus. A hamlet, to be such, must have a common name that comprehends all the single farms within it, though they may have their own separate names as well, often with 'Lower' or 'Higher' or a family name added to that of the hamlet.

Hamlets and farms may be the most anciently inhabited sites in the landscape, though the precise sites of the houses may have shifted over the centuries. A good site may have been inhabited for two or three millennia. Some hamlets were certainly separate estates in Domesday Book; some at least had their own open-field around them, with the strips of the individual farms intermingled. This suggests a communal exploitation and subsequent subdivision of the available land. Such a community may have been planted on the edge of existing farmland or on the waste by a landlord keen to increase his rents. At Dunnabridge on Dartmoor just such a planting was made about 1300, perhaps to man the cattle pound there. Such settlements may also have been spontaneous, with landlord's permission or not. It may also be that one farm became subdivided between heirs, thus forming a hamlet. Most simply, farm may simply have been added to farm as the population grew and more land was needed for cultivation. Some hamlets may have been where the 'smallholders', or perhaps craftsmen, of Domesday Book lived.

Some hamlets (and indeed some single farms) have churches attached. These are 'church towns', where the church, a farm, a few cottages, are the centre of a parish of widely-scattered farms and other hamlets. Clayhidon, Sheldon, Luppitt in the Blackdowns, Cheldon near Chulmleigh and Halwell in the South Hams, amongst so many others, are like this. At Venn Ottery, the church stands almost within the farmyard of Barton Farm. A glance at the tithe map shows that Halwell and Morleigh contain within their parish boundaries what was left after the surrounding parish boundaries had reached what was originally hilly upland common land. Both are 'new' parishes, created out of this waste with no real village. Morleigh means 'the clearing in the moor'. In other places, manor house and church adjoin, perhaps for the convenience of the lord of the manor. The costs of building a church were partly his.

The 18th century saw a further taking-in of the waste. Villagers had the right—'squatters' right'—to build cottages on waste land, provided they could get a chimney up and a fire lit in 24 hours. Jolly Lane Cottage in Hexworthy orginated in this way. Once the house was built, a few fields were taken in, and there was the makings of a farm, for which rent would be paid. This process was probably at work wherever there was waste land, around commons or on the verges of roads, but it is very noticeable in the valleys of the Blackdown Hills, where landlords granted leases for cottages 'lately erected on the waste'. This was the penultimate phase of the taking-in of the waste that had begun when man first became a settled farmer. The last phase on a large scale was the parliamentary enclosure of the hill-top wastes all over the county, at a time at the turn of the 18th century, during the wars against France, of very high corn prices and increasing population.

Fields are of course also part of the landscape. The three- or four-acre hedged 'parks', as they are often called, are absolutely characteristic of Devon. Not all, by any means, are ancient. Around some of the big villages is often a rough circle of land that is or was without farms or farm buildings. Beyond this, farms, hamlets and their fields make up the rest of the parish. This rough circle probably enclosed the land of the village farms, those that lay within the village site. Frequently the fields within this area form a very regular pattern with parallel sides, forming a series of elongated rectangles. They look like the classic open-field strips of the textbooks, and that may be just what they are, though now enclosed by banks.

It is clear that open-fields existed widely in medieval Devon, and that round many villages were large areas of more or less hedgeless land, divided into furlongs and strips. Farmers owned widely scattered strips in these common fields. Braunton Great Field is still farmed in

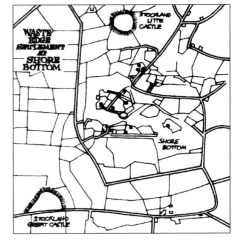

42 *Braunton medieval Great Field, showing some of its 312 acres divided into 86 strips and 21 named furlongs, cultivated by four to five men, owned by 23 landowners. In 1840 there were 448 strips, 46 landowners and 62 cultivators. One of only two places in the country where this ancient system of land division survives. No serious attempt was ever made to 'enclose' it as a whole.*

this way, a survival of the past. It has its strips and 'landscores', unploughed low boundary banks, and furlong names. In some ways it is a better relic of open-field farming than the more famous Laxton, though in Devon the full logic of the open-field system does not seem to have been reached. Maps and documents provide evidence of the system from all over the county, yet at least by the 18th century, Braunton and a few other places apart, Devon had no open-fields left. At some time they had given way to the hedged landscape of today.

One factor which may have led to this disappearance was the abundance of waste in Devon. At one time, probably every parish had its furzy common, difficult or unrewarding to plough, where animals could be grazed, firewood cut, and stone or sand dug freely. Farmers' livestock could be summered on the common, leaving the open-fields free of stock. In contrast, in the Midlands, with progressively less and less common land to each parish as the population grew, the rules of the village laid down that all the village livestock should have access to all the arable strips after harvest, and to all the fallow land. No such rigidity seems to have existed in Devon, and thus it was possible for exchange and enclosure of the strips to take place without harming one's neighbours. On the land so enclosed, Devonshire farmers applied themselves to become, it seems, amongst the best farmers in the country, whilst the Midland peasant was still limited by the restrictions of partly communal agriculture.

This enclosure of common land, creating in part the present landscape, took place at different times in different parts of the county. Where pastoral farming predominated, as in east Devon at Axminster, the strips were enclosed early, in the 13th century, to provide enclosed fields for the grazing of livestock. Some meadowland, here reserved for making hay, was left in unenclosed 'doles' and strips for centuries. The need to enclose this was minimal. Where arable farming predominated, as in the South Hams at Stoke Fleming, enclosure seems to have been delayed until the 15th century, when a declining population and abandoned land made a consolidation of strips easy. Until then corn growing in unenclosed strips was common practice, and presented few difficulties, so, with less emphasis on livestock, there was less need to enclose. At Kenton in the Exe valley, the process was delayed until the late 16th and early 17th centuries. Kenton was an arable parish with markets for corn in Exeter and Topsham. What happened on the wet clays of central Devon or around the Taw and Torridge estuary is uncertain. A good deal of the wetter and higher land may never have been under the open-field system. Braunton Great Field, famous in the past for its arable crops, remains a relic of what was once commonplace in the arable areas of the county. Walking over it is a journey into the past.

43 *Late medieval longhouse, Gidleigh.*

The impulse for the village people to farm communally was long dying. At East Portlemouth, Rickham Common was enclosed from waste, probably in the 18th century, and divided amongst the local farmers into small unenclosed strips, perhaps for the growing of furze. These survived as late as 1840. In Devon such land was often cropped for a few years and then allowed to revert to rough grazing again for another 20 years or so, until demand improved and further cropping was indicated. This was 'outfield' cultivation, in contrast to the 'infield' of permanent cultivation. Traces of outfield banks can still be seen on upland commons, but much outfield must now be in permanent cultivation. The 'many hills that man may plough' referred to in a Saxon charter of 958 for Sampford Peverell must relate to this practice.

Woodland still occupies the steeper and less accessible corners of the landscape. If the place-name suffixes 'shaw', 'beare' and 'wood' are any indication, then woodland in Devon was once extensive. Some surviving woodland is certainly ancient. Harpford Wood, near Sidmouth, was once Chettisholt. The first syllable of this name derives from the Celtic word for wood, indicating an existence of at least 13 centuries. Morchard, in Morchard Bishop and Cruwys Morchard, is the 'great wood' in the same language. Some woodland still surviving is named in monastic records of the 16th century. Once all woodland was carefully managed, felled or coppiced regularly for charcoal, tanning or firewood faggots.

Last to fill out the landscape of the county were the towns. Domesday Book records four towns in Devon in 1086: Exeter, Barnstaple, Totnes and Lydford. Exeter's urban origins are Roman at least; the others can trace their history to King Alfred's defensive 'burhs'. At Lydford, the Saxon ditch and the layout of the old town can still be seen but, though a castle and the stannary prison were built there, Lydford soon declined to the village it is today. At Halwell what may be the remains of Alfred's burh are still visible on the hill-top; it too is now a small village. Totnes, which took Halwell's place, and Barnstaple, which replaced Pilton, were

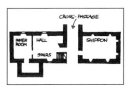

44 *Ground plan of a Devon longhouse.*

45 *Lydford was one of the four Devon places listed as 'burghs' or 'towns' in King Alfred's 'Burghal Hidage' and in Domesday Book. The town ditch and bank straddle the village street. At the far end of the street the squared keep of the castle/Stannary prison can be seen and beyond that are the church and the mound of the earliest castle at the end of the spur.*

46 *Blade of a long-handled Devon shovel.*

thriving boroughs and centres of trade from an early date. Small towns and other settlements, which defy a precise definition as town or village, are a feature of the Devon landscape. The origins of these appear to belong to the later medieval period and are dealt with elsewhere.

Much of the landscape of the county today—hedges, fields, farm-steads, hamlets— must be five or six hundred years old at the very least. The origins of these settlements, their chronology and the relationships between them, remain problematical. Here and there 18th- and 19th-century enclosures on the upland commons have left their mark, but generally this is a landscape made by medieval peasants to suit their own needs. Elsewhere in England landlord and yeoman farmer created a different landscape to suit the needs of industrial England, and the new farming. Devon's countryside is pre-industrial, where folk have lived, worked and died for many millennia. If this is so, then the history of Devon's landscape differs from much of the rest of England, and this in turn may explain its peculiar character and charm.

7

Medieval Devon

Each of the 983 places mentioned in Domesday Book was in some sense a manor. There is nothing, apart from a comparative scarcity of manorial documents, to show that the manor, that great medieval institution, did not develop as fully in Devon as elsewhere in England. It is clear that the earls of Devon and the abbots of Tavistock at least exercised to the full their rights as feudal magnates. In fact the monks at Tavistock were still actively running their own estates and lands in 1500, when in the rest of England landlords were largely leasing their estates to tenants. There were still serfs on the Tavistock estates after the Dissolution of the Monasteries, and even in the 18th century a tenant's heir still paid the 'heriot' or the fine of the 'best beast' to the lord of the manor when his predecessor died.

There was no escaping the manor. In a deferential society with a largely non-monetary economy, it was probably the only way to ensure that all ranks of men had a livelihood from the land or from services, and that the immediate military needs of the country could be met. Many manor courts survived into the last century, and a few still exist today.

47 *Morwell Barton, the country house of the abbots of Tavistock.*

48 *Religious sites, castles and fortified houses.*

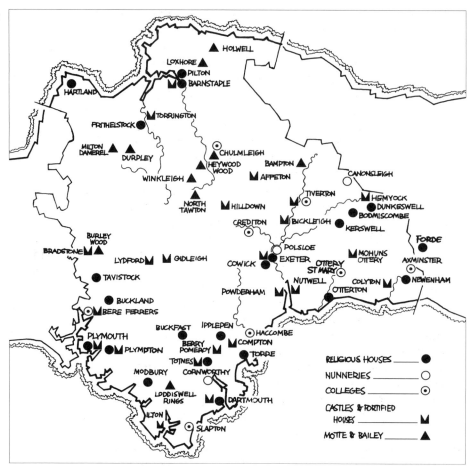

In the small parish of Meavy there were three manors still surviving in 1750, each with its court leet, and such courts still settled local disputes and admitted new tenants; farm leases were often still manorial in form.

Domesday Book makes no direct mention of that other medieval institution, the royal forest. Wiltshire and Dorset had forests where deer were preserved for the royal hunt. In Devon, Adret the Forester held land at Manaton in 1086, and the tenant of Skerraton in Dean Prior held his land by rendering three arrows whenever the king came to hunt; but Domesday Book implies only that Dartmoor and Exmoor were upland grazing areas, where neighbouring cattle were grazed in summer. By the 12th century, however, there was much royal forest in Devon. Forest courts were held; the lord of Plympton and the town of Ottery St Mary were fined for breaking the forest laws. Forest law, administered by separate 'verderer's courts', and designed to protect the rights of the king and preserve his deer, was often fiercely enforced and carried harsh penalties. So onerous was it, that in 1204 the men of Devon purchased their freedom from it—excepting on Dartmoor and Exmoor—from King John for £3,333 or 5,000 marks. It seems unlikely that the whole county had been subject to forest law. It is more probable that some Norman or Angevin king had imposed forest law on large parts of Devon, certainly on the great wastes like Dartmoor and Exmoor, and perhaps on other lesser moors like Woodbury Common and the Blackdowns. The sum paid by the men of Devon was a large one, and they seem to have been largely united in their desire to purchase their freedom, outside the carefully defined limits of Dartmoor and Exmoor. From 1204, the process of clearing the remaining woodland and waste, and the founding of new farms, could proceed unhindered. Within the forest of Dartmoor, tin working was thriving by 1200, and henceforward forest law had to compete with stannary law.

49 *1st Earl of Devon of the second creation.*

Just as it had nothing to say about the forest, so Domesday Book is almost equally silent about the church. Nine places in Devon were credited with churches in 1086. Exeter had four; elsewhere, at Woodbury, Axminster, Colyton, Pinhoe and Kingskerswell, the churches had land, and this may explain the Survey's silence about the other, perhaps landless, churches that almost certainly existed at Honeychurch, St Marychurch, Petrockstow, Christow and Instow, for instance.

Tithe was certainly a recognised payment a century or so before the Conquest. This was a payment to a local church, so it is likely that most communities of any size had a church, or at least a burial ground and a preaching cross, by the Conquest. Perhaps, as at Brentor, pre-Christian sites were consecrated for Christian use. The pastoral organisation of the Saxon church was based on the large minster churches—Exminster, Axminster, Colyton, South Molton, among others in Devon. These served a much larger area than a parish. By the 11th century, however, distinct parishes with clear boundaries were being created, and in each of these the first churches, probably of cob and thatch, were built, to be replaced, perhaps in the 12th or 13th centuries, by more permanent stone churches. A great many churches were dedicated—or more likely, rededicated—

50 *St Michael's at Brentor. A Christian church set within a pre-Christian site, perched on its solitary tor.*

51 *Bishop Grandisson: carved corbel profile, Ottery St Mary.*

about that time, each with its patronal saint, whose day would be the occasion for a feast or 'revel' in the village. By the 13th century it is probable that every parish in Devon was beating its bounds and proudly adding to the beauty of its church through the gifts of individuals, or of the parish gilds, fraternities or 'stores' of local men and women. In due course a 'church house' would be built, doubling sometimes as almshouse, school and parish alehouse, where the 'church ales' would be held. Some church houses still survive today, sometimes still so named, or turned into inns. Occasionally such an inn is still parish property.

As they stand now, most Devon churches, with their magnificent rood screens, date from the 15th century, in theory a period of economic decline. Many, however, have fonts of a much older date, a sure indication of antiquity. It seems that there was enough prosperity in many Devon parishes to permit the rebuilding of the parish church, often on a substantial scale, in the later Middle Ages.

Religious zeal and enthusiasm are also manifest in the founding and building of monasteries. Domesday Book refers only to Tavistock and Buckfast; the one founded in 981 by the Saxon Earl Ordulf, King Edgar's brother-in-law, as part of established royal policy; the other by the Danish King Cnut in 1018. But by 1086 there were almost certainly other religious houses at Hartland and Plympton; Hartland was founded by Gytha, King Harold's mother. There had also been a monastery in Exeter since the seventh century, but this had been incorporated in the cathedral since 1050. St Nicholas's Priory in Exeter, a cell of Battle Abbey, was founded shortly after the Conquest, and the 12th century saw the foundation of Canonsleigh (*c.*1130), St James, Exeter (1143), Polsloe (1190) and Torre (1196). In the next century or so, a further 14 priories or monasteries were founded, the most notable being Ford, Buckland, Newenham and Dunkeswell. The earls of Devon—the distant descendants of the first Norman sheriff of Devon, Baldwin de Brionne—were the most notable founders of religious houses: Cowick, St James, Forde and Buckland. Dunkeswell, Torre and Polsloe were founded by William de Brewer, councillor to Richard I, John, and Henry III. Other founders included the Zouches, the de Tracys and the Peverells. In 1336 Bishop Grandisson founded the college at Ottery, and in 1374 Sir Guy de Brian the chantry at Slapton. These rich families were making their peace with God, ensuring both a resting-place for their bodies and a place of continuous prayer for their souls, and contributing to 'good works'.

Compared with other counties, Devon had rather few monasteries and even fewer nunneries, but Forde rivalled the famous Rievaulx for size, and Torre was the richest Premonstratensian house in the country. Newenham, Ford and Dunkeswell were Cistercian houses, built in remote sites away from the world. If the activities of these abbeys in any way matched those of Tavistock, they provided learning, charity, hospitality and a refuge from the world, as well as examples to the rest of the county of good estate management. At the height of the monastic movement there were perhaps a thousand religious in the county.

52 *Bishop Grandisson: roof boss from Ottery St Mary.*

In Exeter, successive medieval bishops (Quivil, Bronescombe and Stapledon) were altering and adding to the great cathedral of St Peter, demolishing the Norman nave but leaving the two great Norman towers intact. Tiverton, Cullompton and Totnes, rich with the profits of cloth, were building fine town churches; there were Franciscan and Dominican houses in Plymouth and Exeter, and hospitals for the sick and lepers in Exeter, Honiton, Sowton, Plympton and Torrington. The bishop had palaces at Chudleigh, Bishop's Tawton and Bishop's Teignton; he was one of the county's greatest landowners. The monasteries also owned much land, and were not necessarily benevolent landowners. It would have been difficult to escape the influence and power of the church in medieval Devon.

There were, however, some opportunities to escape from the servility of the manor. A peasant could become a free tinner, and then no lord could touch him. Alternatively, if he was enterprising, he could become a townsman, a burgess, and make a living from trade and industry. Theoretically, a year and a day's residence in a town made a man safe from the grip of the manor court.

In the two-and-a-half centuries after the Domesday inquest, many towns were founded in the county, or, at least, many places acquired some urban functions and qualified as 'boroughs'. Many may have been functioning as such long before they were recorded as boroughs in any formal sense. It was to the advantage of the lord of a manor to found a borough with a market, fair, and rent-paying burgesses. Trade and market dues and tolls would increase his income if the town succeeded. Between 1086 and the arrival of the Black Death in 1348 no less than 61 new boroughs can be counted, and the final count for Devon is 74, more than twice the number for any other county.

Some 31 of the Devonshire boroughs survive today as recognisable towns; the rest failed to become modern urban settlements. Many founders were great lords, like William de Vernon, fifth earl of Devon, who founded Honiton, Plympton and probably Tiverton. The abbot of Tavistock did the same for Tavistock, Denbury and Hatherleigh; William de Albemarle was responsible for Woodbury and Lympstone; Richard de Grenville for Bideford; Henry de Tracy for Bovey Tracey and Bow; the abbot of Buckfast for Kingsbridge; and William de Brewer for Axminster and Newton Poppleford. For some 33 boroughs, the approximate date of the foundation and the name of the likely founder are known. Some founders may merely have been regularising an existing situation, as at East Teignmouth, where the charter for the market postdates the market itself.

53 *Carved corbel profile from Ottery St Mary.*

54 *Grooves on Kenton Church porch, perhaps used to sharpen arrowheads when archery practice was compulsory.*

The success of a town depended on its location in relation to other towns, and to the size and wealth of its hinterland. In Devon, the flourishing wool and cloth trades, tin mining, seaborne trade, difficult communications and a versatile husbandry made the chances of success perhaps greater than elsewhere. However, it is unlikely that Wiscombe and Whitford in east Devon—the one a great house, the other a hamlet today—ever became urban or self governing in any way. Some, like West Alvington and Dodbrooke in Kingsbridge, and Bridgetown Pomeroy in Totnes, were eventually absorbed by larger neighbours. Other places, seemingly likely candidates for borough status, such as Ottery St Mary and Colyton, never seem to have acquired the title officially, though both apparently had markets by 1226. Silverton was a borough; adjoining Thorverton, equally large, was not. Their appearance today would not lead one to suspect such a distinction.

At Honiton the outline of what was perhaps really a 'new town', with its narrow 'burgage plots' behind each house, and its clearly delineated boundary, can be seen on either side of the old Roman road. Much the same can be seen at Bow, South Zeal, Chillington and Newton Poppleford (whose name means 'the new town at the pebble ford'). Honiton, like Newton Abbot, Tiverton, Tavistock and Bideford, succeeded; others, like Newton Poppleford and Aveton Gifford, remained villages, though they may have fulfilled an urban function in the past. Local trade and industry flourished best in a borough, away from the restrictions of the manor. Fifty-three of these boroughs are first recorded between 1200 and 1300, and only 15 from after 1300, of which seven occur first after the Black Death. Clearly, 13th-century landowners encouraged the emergence of boroughs and their tenants to turn to industry and commerce, although many so-called burgesses might still farm some land.

It seems that what elsewhere might have remained a large village, often acquired borough status. Devon had the greatest density of boroughs, in the country, as well as the greatest numbers, with the wastes of Dartmoor included in that calculation. The success of some towns is readily explicable. Ashburton, Chagford, Plympton and Tavistock were stannary towns. Bideford, Barnstaple and Dartmouth lay at the lowest crossings of the Torridge, Taw and Dart, and became ports. Totnes and Barnstaple lay within ancient defences and, like Plympton and Tiverton, in the shadow of castles. Tiverton's castle was the main seat of the earls of Devon and the town stood at an important river crossing. Tavistock, in an unlikely site for urban development, grew up round a monastery. All acquired a market and one or more fairs, some degree of freedom and self-government, and a port

55 *The 'borough' of South Zeal, founded by Robert de Tony of neighbouring South Tawton in 1299 with a market and two fairs, along what was once a main road. The burgage plots and the borough boundary are clearly visible.*

reeve—next best thing to a mayor. Some later were actually able to boast a mayor and corporation, and some sent members to parliament, albeit perhaps intermittently.

The 14th century was one of economic decline even before the arrival of the Black Death, which first reached England at Weymouth, only 30 miles from the Devonshire border. After 1350, only Plymouth, absorbing Sutton Prior, and Cullompton, perhaps supplanting Bradninch, can be recognised as 'new towns' of any size. Slapton chantry, founded in 1374, was both the last monastic house to be founded in Devon, and the only one founded after the Black Death. Nearly half the Devon clergy died between 1349 and 1351; Exeter was one of the worst-hit dioceses in England; the 17 churches in the deanery of Kenn lost 86 clergymen through plague. Tin-mining virtually ceased; lands were left untenanted, and in at least one parish—Templeton—the dead were collected by cart and buried in the churchyard at Witheridge. Many bodies were doubtless summarily disposed of, like the young woman in Hemyock who was buried in the farm dungheap in a much later outbreak.

57 Dartmouth Castle and St Petrock's Church commanding the mouth of the Dart. Dartmouth was a considerable port from the 12th century. St Petrock's may be on a very early Christian site.

The plague, and the ensuing shortage of labour, marked the beginning of the end of serfdom and the leasing of great estates to tenants. But this process took longer in Devon, as has been indicated, and it may be that the opportunities presented by the many boroughs and the stannaries, and the chance to become a free tenant by colonising the waste particularly in the north and west of Devon, made Devonshire society relatively free and less dramatically altered by the Black Death than elsewhere.

Medieval society was dominated by great lords. Their presence, power and status were made patent by the castles they built. The first stone castles—Exeter, Totnes and Plympton—were built to tighten the Conqueror's hold on a potentially rebellious shire, as we have seen. Exeter was a royal castle; Totnes and Barnstaple castles were built by Judel the Breton; and Plympton and Okehampton by the earls of Devon. These were all early; only Berry Pomeroy, begun in 1300, ranks as a later baronial castle. Little-known Hemyock was built by Sir William de Asthorp about 1380. He was a 'foreigner' from Northamptonshire and illegitimate, but was married to a Dynham heiress. From Hemyock he preyed on the estates and property of his neighbours, assembling armed men in some numbers. He was even prepared to confront the Courtenays. The moat and walls at Hemyock were perhaps essential defences, but Compton, Affeton, Bickleigh and Dartington were all manor houses first, with more or less fortification as a secondary consideration. The defensive feature which survived longest was a gatehouse at the entrance to a courtyard. Gatehouses survive at Bradstone, Tawstock, Morwell and Mohun's Ottery.

Devonshire society in the Middle Ages was overshadowed by the Courtenay earls of Devon. Of the Courtenays it has been said 'there is no pedigree in England, and very few in Europe, which can vie with that of the earls of Devon, and unlike most, it is not of herald's manufacture'. There was no lay landowner to rival them in the county. They owned estates all over Devon, and Okehampton, Tiverton and Plympton castles gave them a strong military grasp. Here and there were other important men, like Sir Guy de Brian, of Slapton, Torbrian and Northam, who fought at Crecy, was the 56th knight of the Garter, and an intimate companion of Edward III. But he founded no long-lasting family, and his main estates were in Wales. The Pomeroys were a great Domesday family, but made little mark nationally or locally outside their great castle at Berry. The Dinhams, the Fortescues, the Champernownes and the Mohuns were all feudal families with foreign roots. But the knightly class of Devon was drawn more from the ranks of the freeholders, who held their lands at a knight's fee from king, bishop, abbot or earl. Such are the Kellys, the Fulfords, the Edgecombes, the Copplestones, the Aclands, and the Fursdons, who all took their names from their estates.

By the middle of the 15th century, the supremacy of the Courtenays was challenged for the first time, by the Bonvilles of Shute. Their local rivalry was subsumed into the great Yorkist-Lancastrian struggle. Three Courtenay earls of Devon, and an heir to the earldom, perished in the

58 *Affeton in West Worlington. The 15th-century gatehouse to the demol- ished manor house; now the property of the Stucleys of Hartland Abbey.*

59 *The early 17th-century gatehouse at Bradstone West Devon. A gate- house lent status and was perhaps the last trace of the concept of a defended property.*

60 *Tiverton Castle, the main seat and stonghold of the Courtenay earls of Devon until 1539.*

61 *Berry Pomeroy Castle was the property of Norman Pomeroys from 1066 to 1548. It was sold to Edward Seymour, Protector Somerset, in 1548 and is still Seymour property. The Seymour mansion can be seen to the right.*

Wars of the Roses; Lord Bonville was killed at St Albans in 1461, and his son and grandson fell at Wakefield. Bonville was Lancastrian initially, but both his and his family's allegiance shifted as the political situation changed. In Devon the feud with the Bonvilles led to a fight at Lympstone, and to a battle of some sort on Clyst Heath just outside Exeter, as well as to the notorious murder of Nicholas Radford, the Bonvilles' attorney, at Upcott near Cheriton Fitzpaine. At one time the earl of Devon occupied Exeter and intimidated the mayor and the justices in pursuit of his quarrel with the Bonvilles. Fifteenth-century society was violent and lawless, subject to the rages and quarrels of great men.

8

Good Catholyke Men

In May 1549 on Whit Monday, apparently in response to the introduction of the new English Prayer Book, the people of Sampford Courtenay rioted. They forced the village priest to say mass in the old style, killed a local gentleman who tried to interfere, and marched on Exeter after a skirmish at Crediton. By that time they had been joined by Cornishmen intent on the same end. Exeter was besieged and surrounded. The west gate was nearly taken; the city was bombarded and citizens shot down in the streets. Five bloody battles were fought before the 'Prayer Book Rebellion', as it was called, was put down. At Fenny Bridges; at Carey's Windmill on the edge of Woodbury Common; in the streets of Clyst St Mary; on Clyst Heath; and finally, where it all began, at Sampford Courtenay, Devonshire peasants, probably ill-equipped and ill-led, fought a royal army strengthened by professional Italian and German mercenaries. Lord Russell, the new owner of the wealthy Tavistock Abbey estates, and ancestor of the present dukes of Bedford, was chosen by Protector Somerset to lead these paid foreigners. The number of those who died in the fighting or were later executed is quite unknown, but contemporary accounts do not suggest that they were few. Perhaps the presence of the mercenaries contributed to this bloodshed.

This episode, also known as the 'Western Rebellion', suggests that Devonshire people were not enthusiastic about the Reformation and all the changes that went with it. They were at one with the Lincolnshire and Yorkshire rebels of the Pilgrimage of Grace a dozen years before, and even marched under the same banner depicting the 'Five Wounds of Christ'. Their motives appear to have been religious, unlike those of the Norfolk rebels who, led by Jack Kett, rose in the same summer of 1549, and who seem to have been inspired by agrarian discontent. However, it is unlikely that any of these risings can be ascribed to one simple cause. Rebellions involving thousands must focus a myriad discontents, from simple greed and personal enmity to genuine poverty and religious zeal.

Certainly, up to the break with Rome, Devon seems to have been piously Catholic in ritual and belief. Parish churches were adorned in the traditional way; rood lofts, with cross and images and candles, surmounted the chancel screens, places for music and mystery plays

62 *Badge of the Five Wounds.*

63 *St Andrew's at Cullompton, a fine town church. The Lane aisle to the right was built just before the Reformation by the clothier John Lane, to sing masses in the old Catholic way for his soul and the souls of his family.*

64 *A detail of the Greenway aisle at St Peter's, Tiverton. John Greenway was a ship-owning Tiverton clothier.*

and religious pageantry. Around the church were images of the saints, enriched with the offerings of the faithful. Richly-coloured images of hell and paradise faced the worshippers from wall and window, and candles burnt all round the church, before saintly images and on the altar, maintained by the gifts of parishioners living and dead. Ashburton had eight such images, tiny Morebath five; neither of these was unusual. Each aisle in the church had its own stone altar and separate dedication.

Ornament was matched by ritual. Masses for the dead, paid for in wills and by gifts, were sung regularly in the chantry aisles of the churches. The Lane aisle at Cullompton and the Greenway aisle at Tiverton, both built just before 1530, were there to commemorate the dead of the families whose names they bore and to provide a fitting setting for prayers for their souls. John Lane, indeed, paid for prayers to be said for his soul in 100 different parishes, and the widow Takyll of Honiton paid for masses to be said for her for 20 years, while the knell to mark her passing was to be rung in six parishes. There was 'creeping to the cross' on Good Friday, and processions round the village on the patronal saint's day, as at Tavistock, Hartland, Branscombe and Braunton. Pilgrims visited shrines across the seas as well as West Country holy places, such as 'Our Lady of the Cliff' at Cleeve Abbey, Our Lady of Pilton, and St Urith's tomb at Chittlehampton. There were relics at Crediton and Dartmouth; a fragment of the True Cross, Henry VI's spurs and St Michael's chair at St Michael's Mount; and part of the Crown of Thorns at Bodmin, to name but a few. Bishop Lacey's tomb in Exeter Cathedral was especially venerated.

Village people were deeply involved in all this; these ceremonies and rituals did not just take place at the will of the priests. The wording used in their wills also demonstrates that Devonshire people were orthodox in their religious views. To deny Henry's 'headship' of the church, and to question what he did with it, as William Gowdron and Thomas Bonyfaunt of Exeter probably did, was treason: their views did not coincide with the new reforming ideas of Henry VIII's government and both men were executed in Southernhay. Sir Thomas Dennys, a prominent Devonian gentleman, said 'To be a papist and a traitor be one thing'. A hankering for the old ways, a traditionally Devonshire trait, might thus also be treason.

*V Buckland Abbey. A Cistercian house
begun in 1278. After the dissolution of the
monasteries it was the home of the
Grenvilles and then of Sir Francis Drake
and his descendants, until 1946.*

*VI Castle Drogo, Drewsteignton. A
20th-century 'baronial' castle built for
Julius Drewe of the Home and Colonial
Stores, by Lutyens, betweeen 1910 and
1930. With six-foot-thick granite walls it
is the only castle built in the 20th century
and was originally planned to be much
bigger.*

VII *Powderham has been Courtenay property since the 14th century and the seat of the Courtenay Earls of Devon since the las[t] of the senior branch of the family was executed by Henry VIII in 1539 and his Tiverton lands and castle forfeited.*

VIII *A La Ronde, Exmouth, an idiosyncratic 16-sided 'cottage' designed, built (1798), and orna-mented by the Misses Parminter using ideas derived from an extended Grand Tour of Europe.*

It was not as if there were many ardent protestants in Devon. The Carews of Mohun's Ottery in Luppitt and of Wood in Kentisbeare, deeply unpopular in the county, were one such family; Sir Peter had his own resident Protestant chaplain. He and his uncle, Sir Gawen, were employed by the government to put down the Prayer Book Rebellion. At Axminster, one Philip Gammon, protected by the Carews, was firmly anti-catholic. 'He would as lief confess to a stone as to a priest', he said, and 'the blessing of the Bishop was as good as the blessing of his old horse'. He also ridiculed the sacraments, but had little specifically protestant to say. At Torrington Thomas Bennet, a Cambridge Bible student, began a career that took him first to prison for, like Luther, nailing anti-catholic denunciations to the cathedral door, and then, in 1530, to the heretics' fire at Livery Dole. He was hated; Exeter folk added fuel to the fire that consumed him. Agnes Prest of Launceston was burnt in Mary's reign in Southernhay for her outspoken denunciations of Catholicism.

Gammon was probably not alone at Axminster in his beliefs. Nearby was Lyme, denounced as a 'heretic town' by Queen Mary herself. One Kingswell, a protestant tinner from Chagford, was executed as a 'spy' by the catholic rebels outside Exeter during the siege of that city. There were protestant fanatics, like Christopher Sampford at Halberton, who vandalised his local church, using the altar in his kitchen and a much venerated statue of the Virgin as part of his bread oven. At Harberton and Marldon, Philip Nicholls was bold enough to debate theology in church with Canon Crispin, a noted catholic divine. He seems not to have suffered for this, but the much disliked protestant Dean Haynes of Exeter thought Devon a perilous county for his co-religionists: 'Let the King's Grace look to it!'.

65 *Sampford Court-enay, Church House steps. The west room at the top of the steps was built c.1500. On these steps, much rebuilt, one Lethbridge killed William Hellions a local gentle-man; the first blow in the Prayer Book Rebellion of 1549.*

66 *Henry Courtenay, Marquis of Exeter and Earl of Devon. Grand-son of Edward IV and boon companion of Henry VIII. Executed on Henry's orders for treason in 1539. The only known portrait of the last of the Earls of Devon of the old creation.*

The first signs of change came in the 1530s. Bibles in English were prescribed by the government, but most parishes were slow to buy them. Saints' days were limited, though the patronal feast-days survived. Rood lofts were demolished, wall paintings whitewashed over, images removed, and then sold, burnt or hidden, religious plays came slowly to an end and pilgrimages all but ceased. Church income diminished. There was no obvious opposition to the Dissolution of the Monasteries in Devon. In fact, the people of Wembury and Torre were in dispute with their monastic landlords before 1536, perhaps anticipating what was to come. There were disturbances at Hartland and Bodmin in 1538, and some Exeter women were so incensed by the destruction of the rood loft in the church of St Nicholas' Priory that they drove the workman out of the church; 'they sent him packing'.

Elsewhere, the 27 Devonshire monasteries, priories, and colleges were dissolved without known protest, and their lands were sold to local merchants and landowners at what turned out for many to be a bargain price. Monks were often found livings; nuns could only go back to their families, but all received pensions or stipends of some sort. Some monastic communities, endowed by local piety, had been worshipping God and doing God's work, one way or another, for 500 years, and were very much part of Devon life. If there were no actual protests at their end, there were, surely, regrets.

By the end of the 1540s the pace of change had increased. In 1547 the chantries, where masses were sung for the dead, were dissolved, and their lands and property, once again the gifts of generations past, were dispersed. The protestant Coverdale replaced the catholic Vesey as bishop of Exeter. He preached the new faith in the cathedral, but two attempts were made to poison him. In 1549 the new English prayer book, replacing the familiar Latin mass, was introduced. It was this which apparently sparked off the events at Sampford Courtenay.

It is possible to sense the atmosphere in which the rebellion took place. The church was being despoiled, the old rites and ceremonies were under attack, the religious life of the people had been undermined, officially and deliberately. The faults of the church and clergy laid them open to abuse and ridicule, when there was no official support for them. But there was as yet no real substitute for the old religion: Protestantism as yet meant little in Devon.

All sorts of other matters, however, coalesced to make that desperate outbreak of 1549. Sheep and woollen cloth had recently been taxed, and the tax had fallen hard on Devon. Food prices were disastrously high and inflation was rampant. There was, perhaps, some lingering resentment of the execution of the popular Henry Courtenay, marquis of Exeter, in 1538 for supposed plotting: a number of those who led the rebellion had had links with him, while loyal Exeter had been at feud with him. The rebels asked for different things at different times: for the mass in Latin, for some abbeys to be restored, and saints' days revived; for things, in short, to be much as they were before the break with Rome. They lamented the price of food, the high taxation, the attitude of some priests to baptism, the possible loss of education following the closing of monastic schools, and complained also about the number of gentlemen's servants and their loyalty to their masters. They complained too that the king's ministers had enriched themselves. It is also possible that Protector Somerset's apparent concern for the poor perhaps fostered vain hopes amongst some rebels.

Even the leaders of the rebellion, gentlemen like Sir Thomas Pomeroy and Humphrey Arundell, would have found fault with some of these complaints. Others, perhaps, would have been more sympathetic, like Simon Morton, the vicar of Poundstock, and the Cornishman Robert Welsh, vicar of St Thomas's in Exeter, a wrestler and a skilled archer, who persuaded the rebels not to set fire to the city. He was eventually hanged from his own church tower. Yet other leaders were labourers or perhaps yeomen, like Segar, Underhill and Maunder of Sampford Courtenay. The rebels were eventually dispersed, defeated and vengeance was taken in Devon and Cornwall. Arundell and three others were hanged, drawn and quartered in London. Locally the rebellion was the 'commotion time' and was long remembered.

Mary's reign saw what was perhaps a welcome return to the old ways. The congregation in the cathedral walked out of Coverdale's sermon on hearing the news of her accession. Images at Dartington and Morebath were brought out from hiding, and the vicar of Morebath wrote that they were 'true and faithful Christian people' and 'did like good Catholyke men' again. One man rejoiced that he had heard mass again for the first time in four years. It was a bad time for protestants. Sir Peter Carew stuck to his principles, raised a stir against Mary and her marriage to

68 *The seal of Ford Abbey.*

69 *Henry VIII, carving at Cadhay, Ottery St Mary.*

Philip of Spain, and fled abroad. But the return to the old ways does not seem to have been done with much haste or enthusiasm. Too many inroads had been made into simple faith and piety for them to return again intact.

Elizabeth's reign saw Protestantism return. The cathedral's images were burnt in the close by those who had venerated them, on the dean's orders. The 'stores' gradually disappeared for good; the faithful left bequests to the poor, not to their parish church. Outwardly, the churches conformed, but there is no evidence of any enthusiasm for the new order that had been imposed on them. Occasionally whole parishes, Dartington and Kilmington for instance, were excommunicated for disobedience. Indifference and cynicism tended to take the place of piety. Yet within a century, by the time of the Civil War, Devon was possibly as protestant as any county outside East Anglia.

There were some who did well out of all this. Much of the monastic land was sold, some was given away, and there was thus a major change in the ownership of land in the county. Lord Russell's Tavistock Abbey estates were to be the property of his descendants until this century. Sir William Petre's Buckfast estates followed much the same course. Devon-born royal officials and lawyers also profited; little went to merchants or 'foreigners' from outside. Sir Thomas Dennys, the Rolles, the Carews, the Fulfords, and other Devonshire landed families rationalised or added to their estates, and increased their wealth and status, without doing anything very much to make good what had been lost with the departure of the monks. Education, the care of the sick, and hospitality for passing travellers were amongst the secular facilities which monasteries had provided, and were now left to other folk to provide. Eventually town grammar schools were founded where there had been monastic schools and the Poor Law and lay charity made some provision for the poor. But ordinary Devonshire folk were probably worse off, if anything, after the Reformation: the old religious life of the people, with its colour and ritual, had, with all its faults, brought comfort to many and was now destroyed.

70 *John, Lord Russell, ancestor of the Dukes of Bedford, by Holbein. He put down the Prayer Book rebellion and was granted all the lands of Tavistock Abbey, still in part Russell property till the 1960s. He was president of the council in the West and lost an eye at the siege of Morlaix in Brittany in 1522.*

9

Busy, Crafty, Subtyll Tinners

A description of the Cornish miners in Elizabeth I's reign said that they were 'ten thousand of the roughest and most mutinous men in England'. It was said that 'a tinner's never broke till his neck's broke'. In folk tale, the miner is the dwarf, suspicious, bad-tempered, clannish, plying his unnatural trade in the bowels of the earth, united with his brethren against the outside world by the common danger they faced. In Carew's day, around 1600, the Cornish mining parishes were the poorest in the county, and the life of the miner was wretched in the extreme. At about the same date Westcote wrote of the Devon miner, 'no labourer whatsoever undergoes greater hazard or peril, nor in hard or coarse fare doth equal him, bread the brownest, cheese the hardest, drink the thinnest, yea commonly the dew of heaven, which he taketh from his shovel'.

71 *Brass of a miner, Forest of Dean.*

Mining was a source of work and an opportunity for enterprise and wealth for at least seven centuries of Devon history. Tin was being worked on Dartmoor in 1160, and was still being produced there in the late 19th century, though the scale of the operation varied immensely over the centuries, and there may have been times when activity ceased altogether. At one end of the scale of success was the Great Consols copper mine at New Bridge near Tavistock, where the value of a £1 share in the mine rose to £800 six months after its opening in 1844; which produced 622,000 tons of copper ore; paid a million pounds in dividends; and provided £8,000 a year in royalties for the Duke of Bedford, on whose land it lay. At the other end of the scale were, for instance, the poor whetstone miners of Blackborough in east Devon, burrowing into the Blackdown Hills and selling their wares in Waterbeare Street in Exeter at Scythestone Fair, that was 'all over in a morning'. They were by reputation secretive, hostile to strangers, and 'spoke a foreign language'. In 1840 their workings whitened the hillsides all the way from Hembury Fort to Blackborough Beacon.

The tin workings on Dartmoor are more familiar. It is hardly possible to walk on the moor without tripping over their spoil heaps and gullies, but in fact nowhere in Devon was very far from a mine. North Molton, Charles, Molland, Combe Martin, Rose Ash, Ashreigny, Newton St Cyres, Upton Pyne, Doddiscombleigh, Christow, Brixham, Portlemouth, Thurlestone, Loddiswell, Highweek, Yealmpton, Lew Trenchard, Chillaton and Marystow (to name but a few) all had mines at one time or another, as did virtually every parish in the purlieus of Dartmoor and on the middle reaches of the Tamar.

To begin work, a tinner needed only a shovel, a barrow and a sieve, for which last, it is said, a green turf served very well. The alluvial stream tin was easily dug, sieved and graded in running water, and then carried to the blowing house, where it was smelted, using peat charcoal and a water-powered bellows. The furnace was probably a crude granite structure, roofed over, and lined with clay. When liquid, the tin was run into granite moulds to cool. Wet charcoal spread in the bottom of the moulds served to purify the tin by the boiling of the trapped water. The washing of the accumulated ore, and the blowing of the tin in a 'tide' of 12 hours, were both festive, even ceremonial, occasions with spectators and refreshments.

Once the stream tin was worked out, the tinners followed the 'lode tin' underground, and dug tunnels and 'adits' and 'beams', or gullies and eventually shafts, for which props were needed. Lode tin required pounding, stamping and smelting with wood charcoal rather than peat. Blowing houses were at work at least by the early 14th century, and stamping mills by the early 15th; this may be the time when shafts and tunnels were opened and the lode tin first worked. Pumps of some kind were in use in the mid-16th century, and the need to remove water as mines got deeper may have stimulated both Thomas Savery and Thomas Newcomen at Dartmouth to invent and construct their pumping devices around 1700, though these were not much used until the end of the 18th century. These technical changes may explain the ups and downs of production in the industry.

It is not known when the first men began to turn over the rocks and the gravel, looking for the alluvial stream tin on Dartmoor. It seems likely that this area was worked in the Bronze Age, but there is no evidence of workings during Roman and Saxon times. Domesday Book says nothing of Dartmoor tin, though it records the four North Molton 'ironworkers' and 'blooms' of iron which were due as rent in manors along the eastern side of the Blackdown Hills at Crewkerne and Bickenhall. Mining expertise was therefore clearly not lacking at that time. Records of the working of Dartmoor tin begin in the 12th century. It was being worked—and the mining laws broken—at Sheepstor near Tavistock in 1169, and the offenders were fined by the Justices of the Forest. The tax payable to the king on tin production rose from £20 in 1160 to £100 by 1204. Clearly there was vigorous mining activity at this time.

Traditionally, the early growth of the industry was associated with the Jews. Blowing houses, where tin was smelted, were known as 'Jews' houses'. If this attribution to the Jews is correct, then the blowing house must date from the 13th century at the latest, since Jews were expelled from England in 1290. Joel of Ashburton, one of three partners who 'farmed' the taxes of tin from 1169 to 1188, may from his name and style have been a Jew. By 1200, activity in the industry was great enough to

72 *Engine house of disused tin mine.*

demand a separate organisation under royal supervision. In 1198 William de Wrotham was appointed first Warden of the Stannaries, and in 1201 King John granted the tinners a charter confirming their rights and privileges as 'ancient custom'. From then until the 19th century, tin mining was regulated by the Lord Warden of the Stannaries and his officials.

73 *Tin ingot dredged from Falmouth harbour, shaped to ease transport on horseback.*

The Lord Warden was a royal appointee, the best-known holder of the office being, perhaps, Sir Walter Raleigh. Subordinate to him was a Vice-Warden, to whom much of the actual work was delegated, and below the latter were other officials, stewards, bailiffs, treasurers and clerks. The Warden's job was twofold: firstly to collect the taxes and dues on tin, and secondly to administer the 'stannary law', the law of the tin mines. After attempts to establish a 'staple' or single market for tin at Dartmouth, and later at Ashburton, three towns were chosen in 1305 to be 'stannary towns', where all the tin produced on Dartmoor was to be weighed, assayed and taxed. These were Tavistock, Ashburton and Chagford. Plympton was added in 1327. Twice a year, in June and September, a 'coinage' was held in these four towns in succession. The tinners with their ingots of tin assembled in an open space, and from all over England and the Continent came pewterers and bellfounders' agents, London and foreign merchants, as well as local traders.

Once coined and stamped the tin could be exported. All the coastal towns of Devon exported tin, and there were markets for it at different dates in Flanders, at Bordeaux, Venice, Genoa, Marseilles and the Near East. Tin had a great variety of uses. Pewter, bell metal, bronze and brass all contain tin; it was used in dyeing, for tinning copper vessels, and by the 18th century for tin plating. Initially England seems to have had a near-monopoly of tin, but by the 16th century this monopoly had been broken by the development of the mines of Saxony and Bohemia. Probably a great deal of uncoined tin was smuggled out; there were elaborate and probably fruitless regulations to prevent the movement of unstamped tin. Some was cast into small pieces known as 'pocket tin' and sold abroad at a high profit.

Because of its intrinsic value and its widespread use, and perhaps because it was easily taxable, at least in theory, the miners of tin had considerable and surprising privileges which enabled them to interfere with the property rights of others. By their charters of 1201 and 1305, they could exercise their ancient rights of digging for tin anywhere. A lord of a manor was entitled to a toll of tin if the digging was carried out on private enclosed land, but he could not stop the tinners working. In Devon, no notification had to be given to a landowner of work commencing on his land and, if the land was waste, no toll was payable. At one time it was claimed that these rights extended over the whole county, 'saving orchards, houses and gardens'. Further, the tinner had the right to cut peat and turves anywhere for the making of charcoal for smelting; the right to divert any watercourse to wash tin gravel and to turn the wheels of his mill; and to buy—perhaps to requisition—brushwood and faggots as he wished. Once a man was a tinner (and that was a very broad term) he could not be proceeded against in any other court of law, except for life, limb and freehold. A serf who became a tinner, and who worked on royal land, could not be reclaimed by his owner.

74 *Tin stream workings on Dartmoor near Belstone.*

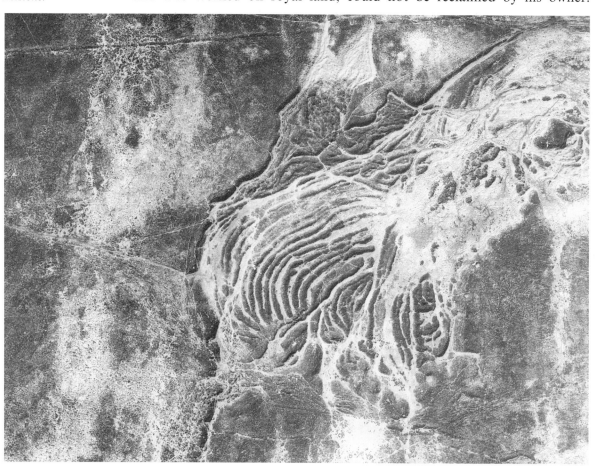

Further, the tinners were exempt from ordinary taxation, and from all tolls and dues in towns, fairs and markets.

Clearly there were immense opportunities here for disputes between tinners and others. Tavistock was a court of 'quick speed', summary justice. Even more formidable was the stannary prison at Lydford,

> where in the morn they hang and draw,
> And sit in judgment after.

75 *Lydford stannary prison.*

This prison was, according to Richard Strode, M.P. for Plympton, 'the most annoius, contagious and detestable place in the realm'. He was imprisoned there for three weeks because he had brought a bill into parliament restricting the rights of the tinners to dig near rivers and sea ports, because of the silting this caused. He had refused to pay the £40 fine imposed on him by each of the four stannary courts, who claimed the bill was a breach of their privileges. Strode was eventually released by a parliamentary writ, and persuaded parliament to exempt him from any further action by the stannary courts. From this case, it has been said, arose the immunity of M.P.s from a civil action while parliament is sitting. Strode should have known better; he was a tinner himself. He was, however, right about the silting. Totnes lost its status as a port to Dartmouth, it is believed, because of silting, and some of Plympton's priory buildings were flooded for the same reason. Strode's case makes it clear that the tinners were no respecters of persons.

Occasionally, the tinners' parliament or Great Court met on Crockerntor, on the open moor where the stannary bounds met. Between 1494 and 1533, at a time when tinning was at its height in Devon, this parliament restated all the rights and privileges of the tinners, and had them printed on Devon's first printing press at Tavistock Abbey. No-one was to be in any doubt as to what the tinners could and could not do in future. The parliament also listened to complaints against the tinners in general, and at first seemed keen to restrict the term 'tinner' to those with incomes from land of less than £10, thereby excluding the rich capitalists. But this restriction did not last, and the apparently democratic nature of the parliament with its 96 elected members proved ultimately to be an illusion. By 1600, 57 of its members were 'gentry', and by 1687 only nine were not of that class. The 13th and last meeting of the parliament took place in 1786. Its rough stone table and seats were removed to Dunnabridge and one 'chair' was taken to Trobridge near Crediton.

Initially, in medieval times, the fairly easily-won alluvial tin of Dartmoor gave a poor man the chance to escape from the bonds and fetters of the manor, and to earn a free but precarious living. But the financial organisation of the industry by 1600, when the tinner was bound by advance wages, or even by wages in kind, to produce a fixed quantity of tin, ensured that the return for his labour was minimal, below that of comparable unskilled workers. It may be that the tinner was usually also a husbandman, and that his tin wages were for summer work only, but 16th-century accounts of tinning agree on the tinner's wretched state, and that at a time when production in Devon was at its height. Writing in 1600, Hooker said that the mines were the third greatest enterprise in Devon, after the land and cloth-making: greater even, at that time, than the sea and ships.

Once capital was required, for digging shafts or installing pumps, the enterprise would fall further into the hands of those with wealth to spare. Many Devon gentry families ventured their capital in shares in mines. The Strodes of Newenham near Plympton, close to the Dartmoor tin, were involved in mining enterprises for eight generations, although their land was always the first source of their income. Later, titled folk from outside the county were involved. The prospects of a lead mine in the Teign valley were bright enough to persuade Lord Exmouth to allow an air shaft on his lawn and a crenellated pump shaft in his grounds at Canonteign during the 19th century.

In 1243 there were 150 tinners in Devon, and this number rose to 436 in 1300. After that there are no certain figures, but about a thousand has been suggested for 1373, and 1,100 presented ore to be stamped in 1515. What is incalculable is the number of labourers who presented no tin, but who could still be classed as tinners. The total figure for 1515 might be as many as four thousand. Then there were the workers in the blowing houses and the peat cutters, who cut the 10,000-odd tons of peat needed for the smelting; the charcoal burners who made it into 'coal'; and a considerable infrastructure of merchants and carriers. A workforce of around five thousand might not be far out. Confusingly, the term 'tinner' could equally well be applied to a wealthy gentleman like Richard Strode, with shares in many tin-works, to a day labourer toiling on the moor, to a small owner working his own claim, and to the owner of a blowing house. In 1515, 90 per cent of the tinners who presented tin to be stamped presented less than a thousand weight (1200 lbs), perhaps four to five ingots. Clearly tinning was still a small man's industry.

The peak of tin production in Devon was reached in 1521, when 280 tons were produced. There had been continuous but intermittent working since 1200 or so, but after 1300 Devonshire production always took second place to that of Cornwall. The 280 tons was worth some £9,400, seven times the rental of the earl of Devon at that date. There was a decline in production after that, to 67 tons in 1600 and to 20 tons in 1629. After the Civil War, during which nothing was produced, there was a revival in the early 18th century to around 55 tons, which was not maintained. The 19th century saw the mines on the central moor, at Huntingdon and Hexworthy and Vitifer, at work. Stream tin from Malaya and Siam (Thailand) finally destroyed this 700-year-old activity.

Tin was largely the prerogative of Dartmoor, but elsewhere lead, iron, silver, copper, barytes, manganese and lignite were all mined. The silver lead mines of Bere Ferrers and Combe Martin were worked in medieval times, and Derbyshire and Welsh miners were conscripted to work in them. In 1086, as we have seen, there were ironworkers at North Molton, and iron was still being produced there in the 19th century, and

76 *Californian stamps, Kelly Mine, Bovey Tracey.*

on the edge of Dartmoor at Ashburton and Holne. The Tamar valley produced much of the world's copper in the 19th century; lead was dug in the Teign valley and barytes at Bridford. A vein of manganese crossed beneath Haldon from Christow and Doddiscombleigh, and was found again at Newton St Cyres and Upton Pine. Lignite was dug at Bovey Heathfield, but Devon has, perhaps mercifully, no true coal in any quantity—there is a small deposit either side of the Torridge at Bideford and East-the-Water. All these deposits offered an alluring bait of great and speedily-won wealth, but it is likely that it was only the exceptional mine which made anyone much money: as much perhaps was lost in optimistic ventures. Landowners were clearly on the lookout for minerals, and there must have been traditional knowledge and expertise available to help them. The availability of cheap labour would have made the risk of failure more acceptable.

Little is known of the organisation of these non-tin-mining ventures in early days. None of them approached the scale of tin mining except for the 19th-century copper mines of the Tamar valley, with their waterwheels, shafts, chimneys, steam engines, railways, tunnels and inclined planes. By then, mining of any kind was highly capitalised, and the work was done largely on a sort of team-piecework basis, known as 'tut' work. It is said that Devon and Cornwall produced half the world's copper in the mid-19th century, but by 1900 this activity had largely been killed off by foreign competition.

There were also other extractive industries in Devon. The county abounds in good building stone. Beer stone was quarried in Roman times, and later used for centuries for columns and arches in churches. The vast black caverns at Beer are still a cause for wonder. Elsewhere, dark red Heavitree stone, green Hurdwick stone from Tavistock, grey limestone from Ashburton and the 'green and purple Dartmouth slates' from Charleton are all excellent building stones, while granite 'moorstone' was used extensively around Dartmoor. Clay was dug for the Staffordshire potteries at Kingsteignton in the 18th century, and Fremington clay was the basis for a flourishing pottery industry that exported to America. China clay from Dartmoor and ball clay from Bovey Heathfield, exported from Teignmouth, were 19th-century enterprises. All over Devon from the 17th century onwards, limestone, quarried from Berry Head, Plymouth, or one of the numerous small outcrops in the county, was burnt in kilns and spread on the naturally acid land. Few places in Devon were far from a smouldering kiln.

In this world of quarries, mines and kilns, the most easily evoked figure is still that of the tinner, shovelling away in murky Dartmoor wind and rain, with the clack of the water wheel, the gasp of the bellows and the smoke of the blowing house for company. With his privileges and rights, he was probably not too popular a figure, and to his neighbours and those in authority he was perhaps seen as one Nicholas Thorning was in the 1530s, as 'a busy, troublesome, crafty, subtyll person of a tinner'.

10

Weavers, Tuckers and Shearmen

It has been said that the piers of Bideford Bridge are built 'on bales of wool'. Such light sayings can reveal considerable truths. In a search for evidence of the wealth and extent of Devon's cloth trade, it might be apt to remark, 'If you require a monument, look about you'. It is unlikely that the fortunes of any Devon town were not made, or at least improved, by the making and selling of cloth. Any good 17th- or 18th-century town house has a good chance of being that of a cloth merchant. More obviously, Blundell's School, the Lane aisle in Cullumpton church, the Greenway aisle in Tiverton church, the customs house at Exeter, the Exeter canal and the 'Dutch' houses at Topsham were all founded or built for the benefit of, or out of the profits of, cloth. Less obviously, the fortunes of the Kennaways of Escot, the Northcotes of Pynes (now earls of Iddesleigh), and the international banking house of Baring were initially Devon cloth fortunes. Least obvious of all is the fact that every village in the county almost certainly had its quota of spinners and weavers, supplying the demands of the tuckers and cloth merchants of Exeter, Tiverton, Totnes and Barnstaple as the case might be.

77 *Blundell's old school in Tiverton. Built by Peter Blundell, a Tiverton merchant, for 150 boys in 1604; now converted into flats.*

78 *The Customs House in Exeter, built in 1680-1. Exeter's cloth manufactory was at its height in the 17th century and the canal allowed sea-going ships to reach the Quay.*

79 *Coldharbour Mill at Uffculme, a relic of the Devon woollen industry. This spinning mill was started by Thomas Fox c.1799, and was still spinning yarn until 1981. It is now a working wool museum with steam engines and a water wheel in good working order.*

Culmstock, in the Culm valley, was a considerable cloth-making centre, with a population treble its present size at one time. In the early 17th century, Helen Manning of Culmstock is said to have employed three or four hundred people, and later in the century Elizabeth Hellings was dealing with London merchants, employing at least thirty shearmen and other cloth workers, had some 46 cloths unsold and was owed over £700 by merchants from as far afield as Coventry and London. These two were not exceptional. Eleven clothiers of Kentisbeare, Uffculme, Broadhembury and Plymtree were owed some £5,000 by an Exeter cloth merchant in 1646, at a time when a weaver's wage was perhaps £15 a year. This sum of £5,000 represents at least six to seven hundred cloths from these four villages. East Devon was perhaps exceptional, but no part of Devon was without its weavers and spinners, and at Blackwell Hall in London, where all the sales

80 *Weavers' cottages at Culmstock.*

took place for the capital's merchants, there was a Devonshire Hall for Devon merchants that could not hold all the cloth they had to sell.

Blake's 'dark satanic mills' are noticeable by their absence from Devon, as are the traditional weavers' cottages with their large windows. In fact, there are mills in Devon: Buckfastleigh, Harbertonford, Culmstock, Tiverton, Ottery St Mary, Uffculme, Hemyock, all had mills—indeed, Coldharbour Mill at Uffculme was working until recently and is now a cloth museum—but for the most part the Devon cloth industry was in decline before the invention of the 'mules', 'spinning jennies' and 'power looms' had focused all the activities of cloth-making in a steam or water-powered mill. The Devon cloth industry was a domestic one except for fulling and dying; that is, it was done in the workers' homes, though these were sometimes grouped communally in courts or 'colleges' in the cloth villages. Large 'weaver's windows' were perhaps difficult to construct in thatch and cob.

Almost all the wool that Devon needed for cloth-making came from its own sheep until the 16th century. Devon still has six native breeds of sheep today, but they are all, probably, the products of recent breeding. Only the Exmoor Horn, a short-woolled sheep, may bear any close resemblance to the original breed. So poor was the wool from north-west Devon that in the 14th century the clothiers thereabouts were exempted from regulations stipulating that no lambs' wool, flock or hair should be used in cloth-making, since adherence to these regulations would have ruined them. Cornish wool was known as 'hair', and Pilton clothmakers were accused of making 'cloth without wool'. Fleeces at Tavistock in 1400 weighed less than two pounds, whereas a modern south Devon fleece can weigh twenty.

Cloth-making for home use must have been practised in the county from the earliest times. The records show that both wool and cloth were exported from the South-West by the 13th century. Rough Cornish 'burrels' were sent to Winchester as early as 1181, perhaps for the use of the poor, and 20 sacks of wool were exported from Dartmouth in 1273. Ford, Buckfast, Torre and Newenham abbeys all exported wool.

The invention of the water-powered fulling mill was a great spur to cloth-making in the county. Fulling, or 'tucking' as it is called in Devon, felts and flattens woven cloth, and conceals the weave, to give a good 'suent' or smooth appearance and feel to the cloth. This result had first been accomplished by trampling or 'walking' the cloth, but in the 13th century the process was mechanised and noisy water-powered stamps or hammers were designed. These could be set up wherever there was a good stream, and Devon abounded in these. A small stream could turn a lot of wheels; the Tale in east Devon turned at least six millwheels in its four miles, at least one of which was a tucking mill. Many old water mills are still named 'Tuck Mill', and many more must once have had that function. Tucking mills are first recorded in 1238 at Dunkeswell, and slightly later at Honiton and Tiverton. By the end of the century they had been built at Chulmleigh, Hartland and Moretonhampstead.

81 *Carved bracket, Tuckers' Hall, showing teasel frame, cloth bales and tuckers' shears.*

82 *Tuckmill at Pay-hembury. Here, in the adjoining Rackhey fields, cloth was fulled and stretched on racks and sold to Exeter merchants of the Worshipful Company of Weavers, Tuckers and Shearmen for dying and shearing. The company's hall survives in Fore Street. Tuckmill was latterly a grist mill and continued working until 1938.*

It is clear that the invention of the tucking mill revolutionised the industry, taking it away from the towns to the countryside, alongside streams and rivers, and perhaps away from the control of town guilds and merchants. A tucking mill required capital, however, and was presumably financed and leased by the lord of the manor as a useful additional source of income. However it was done, cloth-making flourished enormously, and spread all over the Devon countryside. A certain clue to the past existence of cloth-making lies in the field-name 'Rack Park' or 'Rack Hay', adjoining a mill site. This was where the cloth was stretched on tenterhooks, fixed to racks.

There were 38 persons named Tucker in the county well enough off to have to pay tax in 1332. They came broadly from areas where clothmaking was well recognised later, from the Otter valley in east Devon; from around Barnstaple and South Molton; from the Bovey Tracey area; the South Hams; and the Exe valley. The 1534 tax return shows 197 Tuckers paying tax, but by then the name had probably become divorced from the occupation to some extent, and the basis of assessment may be different.

Tucking mills helped to cause a great surge in the export of Devon cloths. Initially, probably, the cloth was made for the local market, but England's climate and high-quality wool produced cloth for which there was a great demand abroad. In 1380 Devon's contribution to this trade was no more than three to four hundred cloths, compared with a total for the country of between thirty and forty thousand. By 1430, Devon contributed between one and two thousand cloths out of a total of fifty to sixty thousand. By 1500, 8,000 cloths were exported from Devon out of a total of 81,000, ten per cent of the total instead of the one per cent of 1380.

From then until the middle of the 18th century, cloth-making flourished in Devon. Wars interrupted exports, but there was always the home trade, probably as much as three times the export market in the country as a whole. By 1686 Exeter alone was exporting 114,000 pieces of serge, rising to 365,000 in 1710, worth some £450,000. In 1620 Exeter's customs returns were only less than those of London and Hull, and most of this must have come from cloth. Cloth helped to make Exeter into the third or fourth most prosperous town in the country in 1524, a position it retained until well into the 17th century. In 1400 it had ranked only twenty-third.

To attain and to maintain their position, Devon cloth-makers had to be innovators. Between 1500 and 1700, there was continuous change in the types of cloth produced, and considerable specialisation within the county. In the 16th century Devon was noted for its kerseys, sometimes known as 'Devonshire dozens' (12 yards instead of the 24 yards of broad-cloth). Crediton and Tiverton kerseys were considered the best. The Tamar valley produced 'Tavistocks', the South Hams 'straits' and 'narrow whites'. These last three were all cheap, poor-quality cloths. North Devon pro-duced 'russets' and 'cottons' (so-called), and later 'Barnstaple bays', and, by the end of the 17th century, Spanish cloth, made out of part Spanish wool, became popular. The Culm valley seems to have specialised in this.

The greatest change came with the introduction of the 'new draperies' at the beginning of the 17th century. These were 'serges' or 'perpetuanos', fine, hardwearing, long-lasting cloths, as the name indicates. Their quality and popularity seems to have depended on the fact that they were a combination of woollens and worsteads, that is, the weft was carded, short-stapled, 'woollen' thread, whereas the warp was combed, long-stapled, 'worsted' thread. Devon sheep seem then to have been largely short-woolled, and so in order to produce these cloths it was necessary to import large quantities of long wool from other parts of England and Ireland. But by the 18th century Devon fleeces were largely long-woolled, as they are today.

The new draperies, the serges and perpetuanos, made Exeter prosperous, and made the individual fortunes of the Barings, Kennaways and their fellows. It has been calculated that the annual sales of cloth in Exeter in 1710 were worth two million pounds. This is for Exeter *alone*: Plymouth and Dartmouth also exported cloth, and Tiverton, Crediton, Totnes and Barnstaple were, or had been, other centres of the cloth trade. Tiverton had 56 tucking mills in 1730, and Tiverton cloth merchants were immensely rich and powerful, in total political control of their town. Daniel Defoe described Devon as 'full of great towns and those towns so full of people and those people so universally employed in trade and manufacture, that not only can it not be equalled in England, but perhaps not in Europe!'.

Down near the Exe, on Exe Island, outside the city walls, the river had been diverted to power the numerous water wheels in the tucking mills. This was the industrial heart of Exeter: the elegant 17th-century customs house, the cloth-workers' pub, the *Bishop Blaize*, named for their patron saint, and the canal basin, where cargoes were loaded and unloaded into the lighters, and weighed at the King's Weigh Beam on the

83   *The 'Bishop Blaize'.*

X *Saltram House, Plymstock. One of Devons three 'great' houses built largely in the mid-18th century by the Parkers, Earls of Morley. The Parkers, like the Bampfyldes, Lords Poltimore, originated in the mining town of North Molton.*

X *H.M.S.* Bellerophon *reduced to a prison hulk at Devonport. In her prime she took the Emperor Napoleon to exile in St Helena.*

XI *Teignmouth Bridge was built in 1827. This avoided both Haldon Hill and a detour through Newton Abbot on the way to Torquay.*

quay. The canal, perhaps the first modern canal in the country, had been begun by the city council in 1540 and was complete by 1715. Without it, the river being barred by Countess Wear, goods could only be unloaded at Topsham. All around the river on any open ground were close-set racks for stretching the cloth. From the 15th century, Exeter clothiers ruled their industry from Tuckers' Hall in Fore Street.

The cloth-workers' houses were huddled into the southern quarters of the city, around St Mary Steps, St Edmund and All Hallows on the Wall, and in St Sidwell's. At what was once known as Carfax, where South Street and Fore Street meet, was the

84 *'Tudor House' in Tudor Street, Exeter, was built c.1660, on Exe Island, once the industrial heart of Exeter.*

> large market house set on stone pillars where they lay their serges. Just by it another walk with pillars which is for the yarn. The whole town and country is employed for at least twenty miles around in spinning, weaving, dressing and scouring, fulling and drying of the serges. It turns the most money in a week of anything in England, one week with another £10,000, sometimes £15,000. As Norwich is for coapes, callamancos and damasks, so this is for serges.

This is the traveller Celia Fiennes writing in 1697; she was clearly vastly impressed. Forty years later Defoe valued it at 'sixty to seventy to eighty and sometimes a hundred thousand pounds a week'.

There was clearly great wealth in Exeter and in the county as a whole, but certainly in the city it was badly shared. In Tudor times, it appears that the spinners, weavers and tuckers were independent, selling their products at market prices, in town market-places or to travelling 'broggers'. But the making of serges, labour-intensive and unregulated in any way, led to the hiring-out of looms by the clothier and to the payment of wages sometimes as 'truck' and to the introduction of piece-work. This is clearly what happened, for instance, at Tiverton. Even in rural Modbury one clothier owned 100 looms, and yarn jobbers in north and west Devon controlled the work of countless country spinners. However, in the later 18th century there was still a class of self-employed master weavers and combers, with its own looms, comb shops and warping linneys.

The employed cloth-workers were poorly paid. Most were skilled, but few got more than labourers' wages, and these declined in real terms once corn prices started to rise after about 1760. In Tiverton and Exeter the wool combers and weavers formed illegal workmen's clubs to bargain together for better wages. Occasionally

85 *A pack saddle. With its various fittings this carried everything on the farm and down the lanes. Carts and wagons were not common in the county till the 19th century.*

86 *Beckford packhorse bridge over the river Yarty.*

87-8 *John and Joan Greenway, St Peter's Church, Tiverton. John was a Tiverton clothier, who, like his contemporary John Lane of Cullompton, added an aisle to his local church.*

the poor rioted, especially when bread prices rose. All the Culm valley cloth towns and villages rioted in 1766, and in 1796 and after there were bread riots in Exeter and elsewhere. Exeter had a regular garrison at this time, partly to maintain order.

From the reign of Charles II, the frequent wars with France dislocated trade, and Exeter shipping was easy prey for French ships in the Channel. Indeed, the French burnt Teignmouth in 1690. War meant a drop in total demand, a slump, and the effect on employment was surely disastrous. By 1700, Exeter was forced to build a poor house and to found a Corporation for the Poor. This institution was itself sometimes to be in debt and unable to cover its costs. In bad times the city subsidised the price of coal for the poor. It has been calculated on this basis that 70 per cent of the population of Exeter were 'poor' in 1671, and it is unlikely that there were fewer a century later.

Exeter's trade and industry was to some extent dominated by a class that made up perhaps a tenth of the population. Many of this class were members of the Worshipful Company of Weavers, Tuckers and Shearmen. This group was powerful enough in the early 17th century to defy the monopoly of the great Merchant Adventurers Company in London, and to make sure in 1698 (with the assistance of merchants of other counties) that the manufacture of cloth in Ireland should be forbidden by parliament. Irish wool was needed in Devon, and Irish-made cloth would have threatened Exeter's prosperity. The poor cloth-workers of All Hallows on the Wall and St Sidwell's did not have much of a chance against such powerfully entrenched interests.

Eventually, by the end of the 18th century, competition from, first, the Norwich 'stuffs' and, later, from Yorkshire's steam-powered mills and new machinery, and later still from Lancashire cotton, killed the Exeter trade and industry. The country was producing vastly more cloth as a whole, but Exeter's share was minimal. The trade did not survive the Napoleonic wars. Elsewhere in Devon, however, it survived. In 1838 there were still 39 spinning mills in the county. Large mills had been built at Uffculme, Ottery St Mary, Harberton, Buckfastleigh and Tiverton, but ultimately even these proved uncompetitive.

Much Devon cloth was bought by the East India trade and sold at a low price in the East. At Ashburton, after 1841, political control of the borough and its parliamentary seat was in the hands of the Jardines and the Mathesons, still today great commercial names in the Far East. Six members of their firm or family were M.P.s for the town. Jobs in return for votes was the bargain, but that was more or less all that kept the Devonshire cloth industry alive. Dartington, Buckfastleigh, and Tiverton still produce textiles. Coldharbour Mill in Uffculme, still water- and steam-powered in part, only closed in 1981, to reopen as a wool working museum with two steam engines in working order. Once it spun the Khaki yarn for Fox's 'puttees'. Its 180-year life was perhaps in part due to the thrift, good business sense and public spirit of the Quaker Fox family of Wellington. Cloth made Devon a rich county for three centuries.

11

Traders, Sea Dogs and Privateers

Devon's two coasts and dozen or so rivers have linked its history inextricably with the sea. Some forty towns or villages make or have made a living from trading, shipbuilding, fishing, the navy, smuggling or 'the seaside'. Probably more folk in Devon earned a living directly or indirectly from the sea than in any other county.

89 *Tudor ship.*

The sea also made Devon strategically and politically important to the nation as a whole. Between Lands End and the Isle of Wight there were really only four deepwater ports that provided good anchorages for the fleet and were free of hazards. Falmouth and Fowey were perhaps too far west, but Dartmouth initially, and later Plymouth as ships grew larger, provided safe havens for big ships in some numbers.

Thus Dartmouth became in 1147 and 1190 the assembly point for the large fleets of the Second and Third Crusade on their way to the Holy Land. English links with Normandy became strong after the Conquest, but it was probably Henry II's acquisition of Aquitaine and Bordeaux, as part of his Angevin empire, which made Dartmouth into one of the most important ports in England for the next four centuries or so. Both Dartmouth and Plymouth were well situated for trade with Bordeaux, and Dartmouth merchants thrived on this, combining it, in war and peace, with a good deal of privateering and near-piracy. It was not by chance that Chaucer made his Shipman a Dartmouth man, almost certainly John Hawley, who built Hawley's Hoe as a basis for his activities, and was perhaps the greatest single figure in Dartmouth's history. It is very likely that Chaucer met him. Hawley's principal cargoes would have been wine, dried fish, wool, tin, cloth and salt.

The Hundred Years War with France, which began in 1337 and ended with the fall of Bordeaux in 1453, led to a more or less permanent war at sea. English ships also fought each other. Dartmouth ships fought with those from Lyme or the Cinque ports. Political ends were served too. The ship *Nicholas of the Tower*, belonging to Robert Wennington of Dartmouth, intercepted a vessel carrying the hated duke of Suffolk in 1450. A 'knave of Ireland' then struck off his head 'with six strokes of a rusty sword'. Wennington had been commissioned by the king to clear the sea of robbers, but Suffolk was no pirate, but in fact Henry VI's closest friend and adviser. In retaliation for the activities of men like Hawley and Wennington, the Bretons landed at Plymouth and burnt that part of the town still called Bretonside, and in 1404 made an attempt on Dartmouth, landing on Slapton Sands.

After 1453, with Bordeaux lost and the wine trade thus in decline, Dartmouth's pre-eminence declined until it was revived in the next century by the Newfoundland cod fisheries. In the meantime, as we have seen, Devon had become a great exporter of cloth.

Exeter imported coal, wine, linen, salt and salt fish, and 'groceries'. However, like Bideford and Dartmouth, and probably most other Devon ports, it was an '*entrepôt*' port, re-exporting much that came into it. Bideford and Barnstaple had close ties with Virginia and Maryland, importing tobacco in large quantities and exporting pottery and cloth. In 1731 two million pounds worth of tobacco was imported and three-quarters of that was re-exported.

All this activity required ships, and in 1788 Devonshire ports had 707 registered ships, employing 4,500 men. Allowing for dependents, workers in other trades (such as ship-building and dock work) and the merchants and their men who controlled the trade, it is possible that one man in every five or six made a living, directly or indirectly, from the sea. Doubtless many small ships and barges which were never registered had crews of two or three men. Inshore fishing flourished wherever there was access to the sea. Boats were very often launched off open beaches, and fishermen worked on the land or did other jobs in winter. Every port of any size had its shipyard and rope walk; hemp was grown at Dawlish and Combe Martin specifically for rope-making, and doubtless elsewhere wherever cordage was needed. Smuggling was also a large-scale and often violent business, in the 18th century in particular. Tea, silk and brandy were run in from Guernsey, often with the connivance of those who otherwise upheld the law; smuggling was not seen as a crime.

From the late 16th century for at least three centuries the Grand Banks and the Newfoundland fisheries must have been familiar territory to Devonshire fishermen. Every year from the 1570s up to the end of the 19th century, the cod fishermen set out for the North American coast to fish for and salt the abundant shoals that formed part of the diet for the poor in Devon and the Mediterranean lands. Dried salt cod, crudely known as 'toerag', was cheap and nutritious. The parson of Newton Ferrers described the diet of his parishioners in the mid-18th century as consisting of 'mutton, beans and Newfoundland cod'. Every sizeable fishing village and town sent ships and men to the Banks and some ships, having loaded salt, cordage and provisions for the Atlantic crossing, then took salt fish to Catholic Spain and Portugal, and returned with fruit, salt and port wine. This was a famous triangular trade. Much Portuguese silver coin entered Devon as payment. Dartmouth, pre-eminent in this trade, kept some links with Portugal up to this century. The Newman family of Blackpool near Dartmouth, wine importers and merchants in that town from the 16th century, still own a vineyard in Portugal.

90 *Beacon Hut, Culmstock Beacon, used to store dry fuel.*

The Newmans also once owned land in Newfoundland, and connections with that island and Devon were even stronger than those with Portugal. Many Topsham and Teignmouth men were also Newfoundland landowners and links still exist. Devon fishermen brought their families and settled in Newfoundland. By 1700 there were 200 Devon ships regularly engaged in a trade that must have claimed many lives. The fishery was a great training ground for seamen; new men, 'green hands', had to be engaged for every voyage. Doubtless they signed on in the old *Newfoundland Inn* at Newton Abbot, the *Beaver* at Appledore, or the various *Dartmouth*, *Plymouth* or *Barnstaple* inns scattered over the county.

91 *Sir John Hawkins of Plymouth.*

Dartmouth might dominate the Newfoundland trade, but by Tudor times Plymouth was the first seaport in Devon. This was partly the work of the Hawkins family, William, John and Richard. William and John have the doubtful distinction of having laid the foundations of the English slave trade to the Spanish West Indies, where they were first welcomed for their cargo, but eventually forbidden entry as intruders on Spanish preserves and as heretics. Hawkins and Drake were attacked at San Juan de Ulua in 1568, a foretaste of the official war that broke out with Spain in 1585.

The war with Spain made Plymouth a naval base. A port was needed at the western end of the Channel to intercept invading Spanish fleets, and to give good access to the Atlantic, less hindered by contrary winds than Portsmouth or Chatham. Plymouth was the obvious place, though its harbour at Sutton Pool was small, and the Sound open to south-westerlies. The entrance to Dartmouth was difficult for large ships, and so eventually the anchorage of the Hamoaze at Plymouth, upstream from St Nicholas Island, became the fleet anchorage. Later still, in 1689, Dock, as Devonport was first known, became the great western dock-yard of the Channel fleet. From Plymouth Drake went out against the Armada, and Hawke, Boscawen and Anson set out to blockade the French fleet in Brest and La Rochelle, though Plymouth Sound was not to be really safe from south-westerlies until the breakwater was built in 1841. During gales from that quarter the fleet took shelter in Torbay, and thereby helped to change Torquay from a fishing village to a fashionable resort. War with France was intermittently continuous for most of the 18th century, and the endless blockade of French ports became a tedious but vital routine for the navy. Plymouth was a great 'roaring' royal dockyard town by then, detached from the rest of the county. From *c.*1860 to *c.*1960, before air travel became worldwide, Plymouth was a great liner port, where Great Western Railway passengers joined Cunard, Union Castle, and German French and Dutch liners to travel to all parts of the world.

92 *Drake's Drum.*

The men who are best remembered from Devon's nautical history, the 'sea dogs', came largely from Plymouth and Dartmouth. Drake, the first Englishman to round the world, uncertain of his welcome when he returned in 1580, asking whether the queen was still alive; John Hawkins, creator of the Tudor navy, and Richard his son, who spent nine years in a Spanish prison, and was the third Englishman into the Pacific, are well known. So is Richard Grenville with his fight to the death at 'Flores in the Azores'. He came from Stowe near Bideford, and he and his family helped to build the fortunes of that town. Another Tudor Devonian was the arrogant intellectual Walter Raleigh, a popular hero of the county in his day, with his expeditions to Virginia and Guiana and, eventually, his shameful death in the Tower on James I's orders. Raleigh came originally from Budleigh. His half-brothers were Humphrey, Adrian and John Gilbert of Greenway and Compton on the Dart. Humphrey was one of the many who believed that a way could be found to the spice-rich Indies by a route north of the American continent. He took possession of Newfoundland for the crown in 1583, and thereby founded the first English colony in North America.

Less well known perhaps is John Oxenham of Plymouth, who planned with Drake a pincer attack on the isthmus of Panama, the route of all the Spanish gold and silver. The plan was a good one, but Oxenham was captured and died in a Spanish prison. The Burrough brothers of Appledore were the first Englishmen to reach Russia round the North Cape, but perhaps the least well known of all, and undeservedly so, is John Davis of Sandridge on the Dart. He made three voyages to find the North-West Passage—the Davis strait bears his name—and also voyaged to the Straits of Magellan. He was perhaps the first man to sight the Falkland Islands and made three voyages to the East Indies, the last two

93 *Hayes Barton, East Budleigh, the birthplace of Sir Walter Raleigh.*

as pilot to the East India Company. The Arctic, the Antarctic and the Indian Ocean; only Drake went further. Doubtless there were other men and other voyages of which we know nothing.

Contacts with North America inevitably led to settlement. Plymouth, Barnstaple, and Dartmouth in Massachusetts, and Biddeford and Appledore Island in Maine, as well as Exeter in New Hampshire, bear witness to this, along with many other places: today many Americans return to Devon to seek their ancestors. The 'Pilgrim Fathers' called at Dartmouth and eventually sailed from Plymouth. 'The sea, the sea' might as well have been the cry of Tudor Devonians, as it was, in a different sense and age, of Xenophon's Greeks.

94 *Compton Castle. A castellated façade was added to an older manor house in 1520. This was the home of Sir Humphrey Gilbert, half-brother to Sir Walter Raleigh. The Gilberts still live there.*

12

'The Best Husbandry'

Oliver Cromwell, who had visited many parts of England, said that the husbandry of Devon was the best he had seen. If he was right, then this was probably due in part to the fact that Devon was almost entirely enclosed by his time. The landscape today—small hedged fields, individual farms and hamlets—was probably much the same in Cromwell's time. There was no great extent of open unenclosed fields, though here and there, at Braunton, Ottery St Mary and Kenton, for instance, they still survived. On their enclosed fields the Devonshire husbandmen could farm more or less as they pleased, and entirely for their own benefit, without having to take note of the rules that governed the more communal farming of the open fields. There was therefore every incentive to improve and, by the 16th century at least, there was a good market for food, supplying the tinners and cloth-workers of the county.

Enclosure was made easier by the existence of plenty of common land. The village's cattle and sheep could be grazed on this in summer, thus leaving arable land free from grazing animals and easier to enclose into individual 'several' fields. Further, common land was used as 'out-field', ploughed occasionally as corn prices dictated, and then returned to common grazing. In order to plough the tough growth of the commons and of the 'ley' grass when its turn came, Devonshire farmers evolved a system known as 'denshiring' or 'beat burning'. They pared off the top sward and growth with a plough, paring shovel or beat axe, harrowed and raked it into heaps, burnt it and spread the ashes. This way the 'spine' of turf was reduced to a good tilth. This system seems to have

95 *Pillavin Witheridge, perhaps one of the oldest farmhouses in the county, dating from the 14th century.*

originated in Devon—hence its name—and was in use by the 13th century. Unless 'denshiring' was practised, it was difficult for the old Devon plough or 'zull' to bury the rough grass and turf efficiently. The process added mineral ashes to the soil, but tended to destroy humus. Hand 'beating', using a beat axe, was said to be the hardest work on the farm.

Another ancient practice, perhaps deriving from outfield cultivation, was 'ley' farming. Under this system, grassland was ploughed up every seven years or so; denshiring the land was often a preliminary. The field was then cropped with two or three well-manured corn crops, and then sown to grass again. There was no rigid distinction between grass and arable, as there was in midland England, nor was there any

96 *Lower Tor at Widecombe in the Moor. This was originally a true Devon longhouse with men and cattle under one roof.*

wasteful fallowing of the land. Unless the denshiring was overdone, as it occasionally was, the humus content and fertility of the soil was improved. Only on steep or wet land is there permanent grass in Devon, and in this respect, and in enclosure, Devon was in advance of the rest of the country in the 17th century. Cromwell's remark would seem justified.

At least by the 17th century, Devon farmers used all sorts of manures on their enclosed fields. To sweeten the naturally acid soils, they used sea sand or lime. Sand from the north coast of the peninsula is largely broken shell, naturally calcareous. This was taken in horseloads from the beaches and spread many miles from the sea. Medieval Tavistock monks transported sand 14 miles, and there were contractors who made a business of it. Sand was used all over the South Hams, and round the Taw and Torridge as far inland as Holsworthy and Rose Ash. In east Devon calcareous marl was dug and spread on the land and, by the 17th century, limestone from Berry Head and Plymouth and elsewhere supplied kilns up and down the creeks and estuaries, and inland too. Seaweed, soap ashes and, above all, dung very carefully conserved, were all used. 'Night soil' from towns was also valuable for this purpose.

In the Middle Ages barley, wheat, rye and large and small oats had all been grown. Rye for bread was disappearing by the 17th century, the poor ate barley bread, and wheaten bread was no longer a luxury just for the rich. Yields were good, where they can be measured—as they have been for the Tavistock estates—as high or higher as those of more traditional corn-growing areas. Peas and beans were common crops. Flax was grown during the 18th century in east Devon, for the Crewkerne linen industry. Hemp was grown for rope and net making at Combe Martin and elsewhere. As early as the 17th century there was a market in Exeter for grass seeds, notably 'Devon eaver' or ryegrass; white clover was indigenous, and broad red clover was a new crop in the 17th century.

The climate, early enclosure and 'ley' farming probably always ensured that the keeping of livestock was more important than the growing of corn. Devon today has two breeds of cattle of its own and six breeds of sheep. The huge orange 'South Devon' or 'South Hams' cattle may have been developed as plough oxen in the corn-growing South Hams. The Red Devon comes traditionally from the north of the county; the founders of the breed were the Quartly family of Molland. A mid-18th-century enquiry reveals traces of the first breed around Kingsbridge, but no evidence, curiously, of the second. These breeds may well have a common origin. Many of the cattle at the time of enquiry were black, perhaps the descendants of the original black Celtic cattle, like the Welsh Black and the very wild Cornish cattle. These would have suited the open moorland well.

Four of the Devon sheep breeds are long wools, perhaps derived ultimately from the Leicester or Cotswold sheep. The two least altered and improved breeds seem to be the Exmoor Horn and the Dartmoor Whiteface, the descendants, perhaps, of the native moorland sheep. It seems likely that every farm had some sheep, some of which would, by custom, be 'agisted' on Dartmoor and Exmoor in the summer, or on other commons: 'drove' roads seem to converge on the high ground.

Pigs were fed to an enormous size for bacon. Fat bacon with very little lean, cider and cream were part of the countryman's diet. Horses did all the carrying work and some of the ploughing. Almost everything on the farm—corn, hay, dung—was carried on pack saddles over a horse's back. There was a local breed of pack-pony and strings of these did much of the carrying work in the county; pedestrians had to take to the banks in the narrow lanes when a train swept past, and carts and wagons were probably still unusual in the 18th century. Until early in this century, oxen pulled the unwieldy Devon plough, encouraged by the songs of the ploughman and his lad. To plough the steep hills and the small fields, the 'one way' plough, that could turn the furrow left or right, came to be used. On very steep land sledges were used, and soil was scooped up to the tops of hilly fields after cultivation.

Farmers paid great attention to their banks and hedges. Hedges had to be cut and laid when the field took its turn to be ploughed. Corn ground needed a good stock-proof fence, and around the grass fields a bank and hedge gave good shelter to outwintered stock. Faggotwood and cordwood were also valuable products. The height of the Devon bank can be as much as six feet, on top of which is the hedge; the core of the bank may be stones, boulders and tree stumps from the time when the land was cleared—some banks are at least a thousand years old.

97 *Devonshire steer.*

Every farm had its orchard, and cider-making is recorded in Devon from at least the 13th century. In every parish a few farms had presses and pounds, and every farmer made his own cider. Some even distilled it into 'still liquor'. Enormous quantities of cider were drunk and sometimes wages were paid in it. In 1750, possibly ten million gallons were made in the county, mainly for local consumption. Farmers also made beer. Orchards were carefully maintained and stock kept out. There were innumerable varieties of cider apple, the two best known the Exeter 'Royal Wilding' and the South Hams 'White Sour'. Orchards were ritually wassailed at Christmas time, to ensure a good crop.

98 *Dartmoor sheep.*

Woodland was also important to the countryman. Firewood and peat were the only local sources of warmth before the 18th century. The undergrowth of woodland was coppiced—cut to ground level—every 15 years or so, and the produce sold for firewood, tanning or charcoal. Timber trees were preserved in the hedges and woods by landlords, and cattle excluded from woodland. Woodland was too valuable; every acre was of use. Furze or gorse was also used as a fuel. In the West Country it was sometimes sown in arable fields as a crop. It was burnt or singed before cutting to remove the prickles, and then made into faggots of 'black sticks' for firing the household boiling coppers. Unburnt, it could also provide useful winter fodder for cattle.

Devonshire farms have probably always been small, though it is difficult to guess at an average size. A common term in the past was a 'farthing' of land, seemingly about eighteen to twenty acres, the equivalent perhaps of the Midland 'yardland'. This may once have been a 'husbandman's holding', enough to support one family. In contrast, the yeoman was farming, for the market, on a much larger scale. Those who farmed land were always the one or the other, unless they had some other trade, as many did in Devon. Two-thirds of the few Devonshire probate inventories that survive show some farming possessions. The 14 recorded husbandmen were worth an average of £56, the 28 yeomen an average of £312. It is probable that the small farmer, the husbandman, was disappearing in Devon as in the rest of England by the 18th century, though he may have survived longer in the pastoral west with its additional and alternative occupations. By the beginning of the 19th century the term 'labourer' comes abruptly into use. In Hemyock in 1829 those who were termed 'husbandmen' in the parish registers in that year now lost that honourable status and became labourers overnight. They had been little else, doubtless, for some time. Devonshire farming is still to some extent small-scale, and many country cottages were the homes of husbandmen who farmed a few acres. The Devonshire farmer remained a 'peasant' longer than most in England.

Most farmers were tenants; they held their land on lease for three lives, potentially three generations of a family. They paid a large 'fine' to obtain the lease initially, and then a very small annual rent. Further lives could be bought in as needful. This way, some families acquired what was almost a freehold, and became prosperous yeomen. Sometimes the 'last life', however, wasted and 'racked' the land. This was the risk of the system for landlords. During the 18th century, landlords began to change to a system of leasing for a term of years, and imposed covenants on how their tenants should farm—how often a field should be cropped, and the manures to be applied and so on.

Despite this, Devonshire farming had a bad reputation in the 19th century. The farms were considered to be small and the farmers backward. There were no Devon improvers like Coke of Norfolk. Turnip cultivation, the improver's panacea, came late to Devon, but by the 19th century horse hoeing and root growing were known, and were fitted in to the arable break between the periods under grass.

The Devon farmer probably survived the great agricultural depression of the 1870s and 1880s better than most. His mixed farming was less vulnerable to cheap American and Canadian corn. Some Devon farmers left and took big farms up-country, and survived where their corn-rich predecessors could not. Perhaps the newcomers' expectations were less and their methods more adaptable. In Devon, in times of low prices, the farmer tightened his belt and stuck it out. Some farming families have persisted on the same land for centuries. The Seccombes have been at Seccombe since 1320, the Reeds at Toatley near Chawleigh since 1602, and the Wills at Narracombe (Ilsington) since 1670. Reddaways still live at Reddaway in Honeychurch, and the Clists have been at Hemyock since the 18th century. There must be many other such ancient farming pedigrees.

Farmers are now, normally, full-time owner-occupiers and prosperous, but there must always in the past have been a great many folk who combined a trade with farming—men like Robert Rosier of Swimbridge, who died in 1644 leaving looms, wool shears, and tucker's racks as well as 15 acres of corn, ten cattle, 73 sheep and pigs, poultry, ploughing gear and two carts. At the lower end of the farming ladder was Richard Sealake of Bishops Nympton, who left in 1588 five cattle, one horse, eight sheep, one pig, some corn, four wood ricks, poultry, a cart and harrows. He had a table and benches, all the cooking gear for his hearth, some pewter, some bedding and his hand tools. His wife did a little spinning. Sealake was a husbandman, worth £22. John Vicary of Farway, yeoman, was somewhat better off. In 1674 he had a house with four bedrooms, a kitchen, a hall and six other store rooms. He had 68 sheep, 24 cattle, four horses, wheat, oats, barley and peas in the barn, a wagon and three carts and two ploughs. He made cheese, cider and beer and had a still. His kitchen had brass cooking pots and pewter dishes, and in his hall was a settle, joint stools and chairs, some cushions and a carpet. Upstairs were eight bedsteads and three feather beds. He had some books as well, and was worth £222. The wealth of most Devon country folk who tilled the land lay somewhere between. The richest yeoman was worth £944, the poorest husbandman £22. All were, in one way or another, farmers.

99 *Bampton sheep.*

13

War Without an Enemy

Some ten months after King Charles I had raised his standard at Nottingham to signify the beginning of civil strife and the final parting of the ways with parliament, Sir William Waller, a parliamentary general, wrote to Sir Ralph Hopton, a royalist general, at Wells. They had been lifelong friends, but were now on opposing sides. Both were loyal to their respective causes until the end of the war. Sir William wrote as follows:

> Sir,
>
> The experience I have had of your worth and the happiness I have enjoyed in your friendship are wounding considerations, when I look upon this present distance between us. Certainly my affections to you are so unchangeable that hostility itself cannot violate my friendship for your person, but I must be true to the cause wherein 1 serve ... where my conscience is interested all other obligations are swallowed up ... That Great God which is the searcher of my heart knows with what a sad sense I go upon this service and with what a perfect hatred I detest this war without an enemy, but I look upon it as 'Opus Domini' which is enough to silence all passion in me. The God of peace in his own good time send us peace, and in the meantime fit us to receive it. We are both upon the stage and must act those parts that are assigned us in this tragedy. Let us do it in the way of honour and without personal animosities, whatever the issue be. 1 shall never willingly relinquish the dear title of your most affectionate friend and faithful servant.
>
> Wm. Waller

Bath, 16 June 1643

Within a week of this letter being written, Hopton with his Cornish army had defeated Waller twice, at Lansdowne near Bath, and at Devizes.

Both men came from the West Country: their tragedy, so movingly described above, was the tragedy of all who took part in the Civil War. Few parishes in Devon can have escaped; the county was the scene of almost continuous destructive campaigning from September 1642 until April 1646. Throughout the war, troops were quartered in Devon, and commonly took 'free quarter' as they willed.

Furthermore, parishes were asked to contribute monthly sums, 'martial rates', for the support of the various different armies in the county. Constables of the hundreds were made responsible for these contributions and were, it is said, hanged or imprisoned if they were not forthcoming. As the war progressed, royalist troops—particularly those commanded by Lord Goring, known as 'Goring's crew'—took to pillaging, taking whatever they wanted, cattle, sheep, fodder, carts, provisions of all sorts. Totnes paid Goring to stay away; but villages could hardly do

100 & 101 *These two friends, Sir William Waller, a parliamentarian, and Sir Ralph Hopton, a royalist, were opposing generals in the Civil War in the west. They were, respectively, the sender and recipient of the letter on page 93.*

likewise, and suffered accordingly. Harberton in the South Hams petitioned Prince Maurice, the king's nephew, who was the local royalist commander, for relief from billeting soldiers. Later, the village people were so enraged and oppressed that they armed themselves and routed a troop from the garrison at Dartmouth. By 1645 these local bands, known as 'clubmen', were active all over Devon. They were villagers who took the law into their own hands, attempting to keep both sides away from their area. In the end, they sided with parliament, since Cromwell's New Model Army was far better disciplined and paid than the royalists. Goring, it was said, had been the best friend the cause of parliament had in the South West. Few villages can have escaped exaction, since the armies crossed and recrossed Devon continuously.

The cause of all this action was simple enough. Cornwall was largely royalist—certainly the leading gentry were, at least. The Cornish infantry were possibly the best in the country initially, and were needed by the king to fight further east. From Oxford, his headquarters, he was intent on capturing London. With the capital in his hands, the Civil War would be won; to get it, he needed all the strength he could muster. But the Cornish, after a brave effort in 1643, were reluctant to leave Cornwall. Their homes would always be at the mercy of the Plymouth garrison while that town remained in parliamentary hands, which it did for the whole period of the war, sustaining a siege of three and a half years and losing, it is estimated, 8,000 men in so doing. At the other end of the county, Lyme and Taunton fulfilled the same role after 1644, and Lyme was never captured. While these places remained in the hands of parliament, the king could not draw on the well of West-Country loyalty. So the royalists made every effort they could to reduce these towns, and to hold the rest of the county for the king; hence the incessant military activity.

Devon like other counties was divided in loyalty, but recent work has shown that amongst ordinary folk there was more support in Devon for parliament than for the King. Only central Devon, the hilly parishes round the fringes of Dartmoor and some parts of east Devon were royalist. Both north and south Devon were for parliament. The latter was swayed in part by the continued presence of the parliamentary garrison of Plymouth under siege but active for the whole war. North Devon was entirely for parliament, perhaps following the example of Barnstaple, the most parliamentary town in Devon, and of South Molton where early royalist attempts to recruit were repulsed ignominiously. The parishes of the Culm Valley—Cullompton, Hemyock, Uffculme—were solidly for parliament, their livelihood depended on cloth and cloth workers everywhere were famously radical in both religion and politics. Few towns in Devon did not make cloth at this time.

The parishes of the lower Exe and between that river and the Blackdowns were royalist. Ottery St Mary was a royalist town, fearful, according to local tradition, of the arrival of Cromwell and Fairfax and the New Model Army in 1645. Their fear was well grounded, the church was vandalised and the army, sick of 'a new disease', were billeted in the town for two expensive months. Tavistock and Axminster were also royalist, the latter burnt to the ground by the parliamentary garrison of Lyme Regis in 1644. Otherwise towns were almost entirely for parliament though, as in Exeter, there were both social and geographical divisions within them. The parishes round the cathedral in Exeter were royalist while the poorer cloth making parishes were for parliament. Local loyalties were fierce and epitomised sometimes by nicknames. Exeter folk from around St Sidwells were known in the 17th century as the 'Grecians', a name still born by Exeter City Football club.

These differences can be partly explained by occupation and trade. The tinners of Dartmoor were royalists; their prosperity depended on the price of tin and the King had the power to fix this. So the Stannary towns of Tavistock and Chagford were royalist. In contrast cloth workers and seamen were almost unanimously for parliament. This helps to explain both Chagford's royalism, and neighbouring and clothmaking Moretonhampstead's support for parliament. Folk from that town were still abused as 'Roundheads' into the last century.

The evidence of these varying loyalties comes from the recorded words and deeds of ordinary Devonshire people, cloth workers, husbandmen, yeomen, shop keepers, tradesmen, merchants, and the like. They had their own independent political opinions. The lesser gentry, conventionally thought of as the leaders of society, were by and large for the King. They were however unable to command the loyalties of their servants and tenants entirely. They could not force them to change their opinions and allegiance. This interesting finding suggests that traditional deference had its limits in Devonshire society.

102 Above left. *Civil War: the march of Sir Ralph Hopton and the Cornish Army in 1643.*

103 Above right. *Civil War: the Western campaign of 1644.*

104 Left. *Civil War: the last campaign in the West, 1645-6.*

The roots of opposition to the King grew in puritan soil. There were puritan nonconformist congregations in almost every town and in many villages. Lyme Regis for instance was described in the 16th century as 'a heretic town' and some thirty puritan ministers were present within the town during its three-year siege. In the towns merchants and clothiers took the lead. The trade they promoted often brought with it from 'abroad' radical ideas about religion.

Initially the recognised leaders of the county—the gentry—were also largely for parliament. This opposition to the King went back a long way. John Rolle of Stevenstone near Torrington, and William Strode of Newenham near Plympton, both M.P.s, had been imprisoned by Charles I for opposing royal policies in the Commons. Walter Erle of Stedcombe near Axmouth (really a Dorset man) had also suffered. There had been considerable opposition in Devon to the exaction of ship money from the whole county. This was a tax to raise money for and to equip shipping, and was legally levied only on coastal districts.

The authoritarian policies of the King and Archbishop Laud, which were thought to presage a return to popery, were also thoroughly disliked locally. A great many of the gentry and townsfolk were puritans, even though Devonshire folk had been prepared to fight and die for the full Catholic faith only a century previously.

There were other old grievances. In 1628-9 parts of Devon had suffered from the presence round Plymouth of the undisciplined army led by the King's unpopular favourite, the Duke of Buckingham. This force had been on its way to fight—disastrously—against the French. Once the Short Parliament met in 1640, after 11 years without a parliament at all, it was beset with petitions from the gentry and the towns citing familiar grievances about trade, religion, unlawful taxation and so on.

Thus far Devon was united in opposition but, once it came to open conflict, opinion divided. It is possible to identify 50 Devonshire men who were M.P.s in the Long Parliament, the parliament with which the king finally broke off relations. Not all of them sat for Devonshire or its boroughs. Of these 50, 26 can be said to have been supporters of parliament up to 1648. A further 16 were clearly royalists. Eight cannot be classified with any certainty, though six of them were probably for parliament in the main. All the royalists were certainly expelled from parliament before the end of the war in 1646. Only three of the parliamentarians survived Pride's Purge in 1648, when those M.P.s not in full support of the demands of the parliamentary army to try the King were forbidden entry to the Commons and deprived of their seats by Colonel Pride and his musketeers. Those three who kept their seats were Edmund Prideaux of Forde Abbey, M.P. for Lyme; Sir John Bampfylde of Poltimore, who was an extreme puritan; and Gregory Clement of Plymouth, M.P. for Fowey, who was to be a 'regicide', one of those few executed at the restoration of Charles II for their part in Charles I's trial and execution. The rest of the Devon M.P.s parted company with Cromwell and the army in 1648. They were not prepared to go to extremes and recoiled at the idea of bringing the King to trial.

Many of the Devon M.P.s were related, each a part of that web of relationships, in which even Cromwell shared, that made up the 'political nation'. The two early leaders for parliament were Bampfylde and Sir John Northcote. Their descendants are the present-day Lords Poltimore and Iddesleigh. Northcote was M.P. for Ashburton, where his fellow M.P. was Sir Edmund Fowell of Fowellscombe in Ugborough, another parliamentarian. He was related to Edmund Prideaux, whose predecessor at Lyme had been Walter Erle, a cousin of Walter Yonge of Escot in Talaton and of Colyton, who was a colonel in Cromwell's army and M.P. for the newly-revived borough of Honiton. William Pole, the other M.P. for Honiton, was also a relation, but a royalist. Sir William Strode of Plympton (also related) was one of the Five Members expelled from parliament by Charles I. Another of these five was John Pym, 'King Pym', M.P. for Tavistock, and the organising mind behind all the opposition to the King. He was brother-in-law to John Upton of Churston, M.P. for Dartmouth, and related to the Drakes of Buckland Abbey, to Sir James Chudleigh of Ashton, the first leader of the parliamentary army in Devon, and also to Strode and Bampfylde.

At Tavistock the two Russell brothers were M.P.s after John Pym died, sons of the strongly puritan Earl of Bedford. One was to turn to the King by 1644. The two Rolle brothers, John and Samuel, were strongly for parliament; their brother-in-law was Thomas Wise, M.P. for the county, and Sir Thomas Hele of Holbeton, M.P. for Plymouth, was a cousin of theirs. He was however an ardent royalist, who gave great sums to the King. Other royalists included the Earl of Bath, who lived at Tawstock; the Seymours of Berry Pomeroy; Hugh Pollard of King's Nympton, a cousin of Northcote's; and Sir Nicholas Slanning of Marystow, M.P. for Plympton, and a relation of the Seymours, who was killed at the siege of Bristol in 1643. He was one of

> the four wheels of Charles's wain:
> Grenville, Slanning, Trevanion, Godolphin, all slain.

The Edgcombes of Cotehele near Calstock, and of Mount Edgcombe, and the Fulfords of Great Fulford in Dunsford were also royalists. The Bullers of Exeter were for parliament. The Fortescues of Fallapit in East Allington (and still of Castle Hill, Filleigh) were divided in loyalty; all these were related or well-known to each other. Doubtless these divisions were repeated lower down the social scale. For all it must have been appalling and tragic to have to decide to fight on one side or the other, in this 'war without an enemy'.

Confrontation preceded actual fighting. Both King and parliament endeavoured to get control of the county militia, the 'trained bands' or '*posse comitatus*'. The King issued 'commissions of array', the traditional authority to raise troops, to his supporters. Parliament passed the Militia Ordinance, which had the same intention. The Earl of Bath tried to read his commission in South Molton and Cullompton, and in both places met vociferous and active resistance. Shortly after that he was arrested by some of the Earl of Bedford's troops, and played no further part in the war.

Northcote, Bampfylde and Prideaux busied themselves raising troops and supplies, and Devon seemed to be safely in parliament's hands. However, all this was changed by the Cornish army, and the first six months of the war (September 1642 to March 1643) saw a struggle between royalist Cornwall and parliamentary Devon. Sir Ralph Hopton, the best royalist general in the West, was detached from some royalist forces at Minehead, and rode with a small troop through South Molton and Cullompton into Cornwall. There he inspired the Cornish to cross the river Tamar and to begin the siege of Plymouth from the Plympton area. Hopton did not stop here, but also made an attempt on Exeter. The city commanded all the communications into the West Country, and its possession was vital. The mayor and citizens resisted strongly, and in the end routed Hopton somewhat ignominiously, after which the Cornish retreated. Exeter was to be attacked four times in the war, three times by royalists.

105 *Stepcote Hill in Exeter. The main road to the West went down this hill and through the West Gate at the bottom.*

To the west Plymouth was in some danger. Its defences were not yet fully organised, although it was easily supplied by sea. The royalists were gathering in strength in the South Hams, inspired by the sheriff of Devon, Edmund Fortescue of Fallapit in East Allington. A great assembly of them took place at Modbury around the royalist Champernowne's great house there. The Plymouth garrison took them unawares, and captured Fortescue and Seymour amongst others, sending them as prisoners via Dartmouth to London. That was in December 1642. There was to be another engagement at Modbury in February 1643, when supporters of parliament from north Devon, intent on relieving Plymouth, were surprised by Sir Nicholas Slanning's troops in a defended position to the east of the town. There was fierce fighting and the royalists were driven off, but Plymouth was not relieved. On the way south, some troops under Northcote had an encounter with royalists under Sir John Berkeley in the streets of Chagford. There the much admired Cornishman Sidney Godolphin was killed.

On the Cornish border things went better for the royalists. Parliamentary forces, under General James Chudleigh of Ashton, were thrown back at Launceston across the Tamar, and the Cornish army pursued them—though checked at Sourton Down in a night engagement, when Chudleigh, with only 100 men, deceived the royalists into thinking that he had much greater numbers by hanging slow-burning match fuse along the hedges—and finally came up with the Earl of Stamford's parliamentary forces at Stratton. There they won a hard fight, despite the hedged hilly ascent of what is still called Stamford Hill. After that the Cornish had it all their own way. They found a clear route through Devon via Crediton, Exeter, Cullompton and Honiton, joined up with Prince Maurice's army at Chard, fought two fierce battles at Lansdowne near Bath, and Roundway Down near Devizes, and by July 1643 had taken Bristol. Behind them Devon fell into royalist hands. Exeter was captured in September, despite the presence of a parliamentary fleet in the Exe at Topsham. Barnstaple was also captured in September, and Dartmouth in October. There followed a winter of relative peace.

106 *Monument in Membury Church to Sir Shilston Calmady, killed at Yarty Bridge.*

It was not, however, to be peaceful for long. The sieges of Plymouth and Lyme continued, now under the direction of Prince Maurice. In May 1644 the Queen herself, heavily pregnant, came to Exeter, and on 16 June her daughter Henrietta was born at Bedford House. Later that month the Earl of Essex, the leader of one of the parliamentary armies around Oxford, made his way westwards to restore the west to parliament and to relieve Plymouth and Lyme. He believed that he would get all the support he needed once he was in Devon. Clearly the Queen was now in danger, and partly for this reason—partly also because he could not afford to lose the West—the King himself pursued Essex, entering Devon through Honiton.

He was loyally received in Exeter, where he saw his baby daughter, who had been left behind when the Queen fled to France. Charles then pursued Essex through Devon, via Bow and Okehampton, and trapped him at Lostwithiel. Essex had not found the level of support he had hoped for in Devon and Cornwall, partly because most of the local parliamentary leaders had left when the royalists took control. His army was forced to surrender, but he himself escaped by sea; the cavalry broke out of the enemy's trap and fled back eastwards. Goring's men tried to stop them, and there were engagements at Hatherleigh Moor and Little Torrington. Most however got away, and some fought their way to Plymouth and Barnstaple. Devonshire lanes must have been full of fleeing and pursuing men that September of 1644.

Once again there was relative peace for the winter. This was the opportunity for the royalist troops to unite and join the king, once the campaigning season began, but the Cornish were reluctant to leave their county. Their much-loved leaders were all dead (Sir Bevil Grenville was killed at Lansdowne), and the Plymouth garrison was an ever-present threat. The new royalist leaders—Richard Grenville, Goring and Berkeley—could never agree amongst themselves; authority and supplies were divided, the chance of unification with the King was lost.

The Prince of Wales (later Charles II) was sent to the West with a council of advisers to try to co-ordinate local action, but could achieve nothing. He was at Bristol, Barnstaple, Tavistock and Totnes at various times. This lost opportunity was disastrous for the royalists. In June 1645 the King was beaten at Naseby in the east Midlands by Cromwell and Fairfax, with the New Model Army, and final defeat now seemed inevitable. By July the New Model was moving westwards. It beat Goring at Langport: his army had been destructively quartered around Taunton for the previous six months or more.

By October, having captured Bridgwater and Bristol, Cromwell and Fairfax were in Devon. They made their headquarters at Ottery for November and December. Their troops were sick and dying, and the weather was foul. In December they besieged Exeter, capturing and fortifying Poltimore, Canonteign, and Fulford, the great houses that encircled the city. Thinking that Exeter was safe, the army set off to relieve Plymouth, and to destroy the considerable royalist forces still in the South Hams and around Okehampton. Royalist morale was low, and

Cromwell beat them out of Bovey and Ashburton, surprising the royalist officers at cards. Dartmouth was captured one wintry night in January 1646, the army leaving their shirt tails flying as a means of recognition in the darkness. The royalists, now belatedly under Hopton's command once more, were beaten out of Torrington after hand-to-hand fighting, and fell back into Cornwall. Plymouth was relieved in March and Exeter surrendered in April. In May, Fort Charles in Salcombe Harbour, held by Sir Edmund Fortescue, surrendered, and in August the royalists in Cornwall finally gave up the struggle. The New Model Army had carried all before it, and was greeted in the end with general relief; the war was over. It had been immensely destructive. The suburbs of Exeter were almost entirely destroyed in the various sieges of the city, Axminster was burnt and there was damage and destruction everywhere. The costs of billeting troops and of requisitioning food and fodder were immense. Law and order inevitably broke down in part, there were casual shootings and violence, but, apparently, no deliberate massacres of prisoners or civilians, no 'cleansing' of towns or villages.

The end of the actual conflict was not the end of disruption to daily life. The history of Devon between the end of the Civil War in 1646 and the Restoration in 1660 has not been written, but if it was anything like that of Somerset or Cornwall, it was an expensive, difficult and sad time for all but the few who actively supported the army and extreme puritanism. Royalists had to compound for their estates, that is, their estates were confiscated until they paid a large fine. The amount depended on the total income of the estate, and an estimate of their support for the king. Many families were forced to sell part of their property to pay these fines, and these lands were often bought by supporters of parliament.

Anglican parsons, more often than not royalists, were driven from their livings—perhaps 160 out of 450 in Devon—and puritans were substituted. The Anglican Prayer Book was forbidden, but otherwise during Cromwell's rule there was toleration of all sorts of religious practices, both within and outside the parish church. Officially, Presbyterianism was the religion of the country, but outside London few seem to have subscribed to it. Sometimes regular worship in the parish church came to an end, and extreme religious sects flourished. Occasionally the parish church was neglected or deliberately damaged.

In time the rule of Cromwell and his supporters became less and less acceptable, even to many who had backed parliament. Heavy taxation; the activities of his major-generals in local government, and the exclusion of the local gentry from their usual role in that sphere; and dissension among the ruling group itself all contributed to this. There were plots to restore the King and many West-Countrymen were involved. The secret royalist organisation, the Sealed Knot, was active in the West. In 1655 Penruddock's Revolt, begun in Salisbury, was brought to an ignominious end in South Molton, and once again Honiton, Cullompton and Tiverton saw armed men in their streets. Penruddock was beheaded in Exeter.

107 *Wynard's Alms-houses in Exeter, built c.1435. They have been converted to offices for voluntary social services.*

It is clear that every part of Devon was near enough to the path of one army or another to suffer in some way. There are still tales told or remembered. In Payhembury, to take one parish, there were the Willoughbys of Leyhill, almost certainly royalists. Nearby at Cheriton lived the Flays, who fled when Cromwell came to Ottery. The parson, Robert Terry, was an anglican, who was persecuted by the puritan Colonel Sanders, who also lived in the village. Both the Earl of Essex and the King led armies near the parish, and the New Model Army was at Ottery, five miles away, for a month or more. In Stokenham Katherine Randall, shot in error through her kitchen window, is remembered; while at Aveton Giffard, Parson Lane built a fort by the river for the king. He had to hide in Kingston Church, and then fled to Torquay, and worked as a quarryman. Later he successfully petitioned Cromwell in London for pardon, set out to walk back to Exeter, and died on the way.

There was old Squire Putt of Gittisham, who was dragged from his bed at Combe by parliamentary troops, and died in his coach on the way up Honiton Hill. More fortunate was Mr. Stooke of Trusham, who picked up a bag of gold discarded by a fleeing cavalier after the fiasco at Bovey. With the start the money gave him, he made a fortune and founded Trusham Almshouses in thanksgiving. There are many other such tales; but most Devonians would probably have echoed the sentiments of the 'Clubmen', or felt with Sir William Waller that this was truly 'a war without an enemy'—a tragedy in which they played a reluctant part.

14

Persecution and Rebellion

Three West-Countrymen share much of the responsibility for bringing Charles Stuart back from his 'travels' in 1660. General George Monck came from Great Potheridge in Merton parish near Torrington, where his ancestors had long been settled. William Morice was from Werrington, across the Tamar but then in Devon, and Sir John Grenville had a great house at Stowe near Kilkhampton. The three were kinsmen, part of the network of relationships that made up the 'political nation'.

Monck claimed to be a non-political soldier. He could count on the loyalty of his part of the army of the Protectorate, and with this at his back he cautiously manoeuvred parliament, the City of London, the navy and Cromwell's generals into a position where the restoration of the monarchy seemed to be the only possible course. In this Monck was ably assisted by Morice, who had been sheriff and knight of the shire for Devon. Nicholas Monck, the general's brother, vicar of Kilkhampton and previously of Plymtree, was Grenville's, and ultimately Charles's, secret envoy to Monck in Scotland. Between them all they engineered Charles's peaceful return, though Grenville at least had contemplated a military rising in the West.

108 *General George Monck of Great Potheridge in Merton parish, Duke of Albemarle. He was the Parliamentary General who engineered the restoration of Charles II.*

Such a rising would surely have been supported. By this time the rule of the puritan Commonwealth and its major-generals had alienated the political elite of the county, even those who had initially fought for parliament. The dissenting ministers and their congregations—and these were a significant and influential minority in Devon—would have been less enthusiastic, but ordinary uncommitted folk disliked the 'sectaries' and 'fanatics', and looked for a final settlement of what was an uncertain and dangerous situation. The gentlemen of Devon had petitioned Monck to restore the Long Parliament, and to bring back the king. After his return Charles rewarded all three men; Morice became his Secretary of State, Grenville was made earl of Bath, and Monck duke of Albemarle and Baron Torrington.

The terms of Charles's return had been settled in advance, though they had to be finally agreed by parliament. Lands which had been confiscated were to be returned; lands other than church or crown lands that had been sold, for whatever

109 *Friends' Meeting House, Spicelands, Culmstock.*

reason, were to remain in the hands of their new owners. An attempted reconquest could have brought more conflict, so the acquiescent acceptance of the Restoration land settlement owes much to Monck, Morice and Grenville. As it was, doubtless some Devonshire families were ruined by the Civil War, and others enriched by it, but most of the county's old gentry families survived. The Yonges of Escot and Colyton, who had strongly supported parliament, were made baronets by Charles II. The royalist Fulfords received no such honour.

The religious settlement after 1660 was not to be so peaceful. The dissenting puritan ministers were perhaps seen as the intellectual and spiritual elite of the parliamentary party. Unless they conformed to the Church of England they were deprived of their livings, nor could they hold or attend other non-conforming services. They could not live within five miles of a town, and dissenters could not be members of city or town councils. It was in the towns, of course, that dissent had been strongest, and the Devonshire towns had been for the most part loyal to parliament. Workers in the cloth industry also inclined towards dissent, and all the Devonshire towns, and a great many of its villages, were engaged in that trade. The Compton Census of 1674 (which if anything probably underestimates numbers) reveals dissenting congregations at Axminster and neighbouring Thorncombe, at Tiverton, Holsworthy, Tavistock, Moretonhampstead, Totnes, Dartmouth, Topsham, Barnstaple, South Molton, Bideford, Plymouth, Bampton and Cullompton. Villages like Brixton, Harberton, Culmstock, Northam and Halberton all had 40 or more dissenters. Those at Culmstock were almost certainly Quakers, whose chapel at Spicelands, five miles or more from Wellington, still survives (though rebuilt) in all its simple beauty. Ashburton and Chulmleigh have surviving chapels that date from this time, and at Loughwood near Axminster there is another of these eloquent, unostentatious memorials to past piety.

110 *Venn Quaker burial ground near Aveton Gifford, a solitary walled enclosure in a field.*

Everywhere ministers were turned out of their livings. Some of them had earlier been 'intruded' by parliament to replace those of too high-church a persuasion. The names and circumstances of both groups were faithfully recorded by Dr. John Walker, the Anglican rector of St Mary Major in Exeter, and by the Rev. Edmund Calamy, whose dissenting father was himself deprived in 1662. Walker records 160 who were turned out of their Devon livings at parliament's orders; Calamy lists 125 who suffered at the Restoration.

In one small area in east Devon the parsons of Upottery, Feniton, Honiton, Offwell, Farway, Combe Raleigh, Broadhembury, Plymtree, Kentisbeare, Talaton, Awliscombe, Payhembury and Whimple were all deprived or persecuted by the puritans. This wholesale exclusion may have been the work of Colonel Sanders of Payhembury, an enthusiastic member of the parliamentary committee for the county. He is recorded as driving out Robert Terry, the parson of Payhembury, from his pulpit on Christmas Day, confiscating his corn and cattle, as well as his Christmas dinner and 'plum porridge'! In 1662 in their turn the parsons of Broadhembury, Combe Raleigh, Feniton, Talaton, Honiton and Kentisbeare were deprived. The latter was Richard Sanders, brother of Colonel Sanders, and another brother, rector of Holsworthy, was also expelled.

After 1662 parish constables were offered 40 shillings to seize a dissenting minister if he preached. Most of these persecuted ministers held services in their homes, or in the open air, but frequently they were informed on, their houses broken into, their goods taken, the congregation fined, and there was no redress possible. Some were even imprisoned: Hemyock Castle and Drake's Island in Plymouth Sound were both used for this purpose. Some of the gentry were notorious for this persecution, one of the most fierce, perhaps, being Mr. Justice Beare of Bearescombe near Kingsbridge. He would have been well aware of the activities of the famous dissenter John Flavel, who was turned out of Dartmouth and preached on the tidal, extra-parochial Salt Stone in the middle of the Kingsbridge estuary, to avoid interruption and arrest. Much depended on the opinions of the local justices, some of whom had been dissenters or Presbyterians themselves, or numbered relatives amongst the proscribed.

Persecution merely strengthened the devout in their convictions and opposition to the government grew.

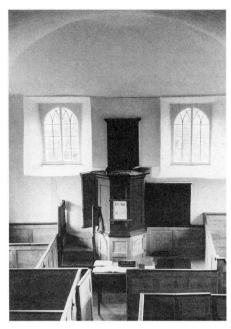

111 *Loughwood, a 17th-century Baptist chapel built in a farmyard. It has a covered total immersion font in front of the pulpit.*

112 *Eworthy Bible Christian chapel at Germansweek, with separate doors for men and women. One of the many chapels of this 19th-century north-Devon sect.*

There was good cause for unrest. James II, who succeeded his elder brother, was a catholic, and openly favoured catholics. He was thought by many to be prepared to use dangerous, even unconstitutional, means to establish a more autocratic and un-parliamentary form of government, which would deprive the protestant gentry of their dominating role in the country, and which would also threaten the established church. Even before James became king, many self-governing boroughs—where the gentry had strong interests—had been deprived of their charters and rights, and royal nominees had been put in control.

Eventually the opposition acquired its champions. The Whig party—broadly speaking, a descendant of the old parliamentary party—and its leaders, the Earl of Shaftesbury and the Duke of Monmouth (Charles II's bastard son), focused this unrest until it sparked first into plotting and then

into actual rebellion. It was long contemplated. Monmouth came to the West Country in 1680 on a progress, to sound out the ground. Everywhere he was met with enormous enthusiasm. The country people turned out in their thousands to see him as he passed from Longleat in Wiltshire to White Lackington House near Ilminster—here he was met by 2,000 horsemen—to Brimpton D'Evercy, Barrington Court (all in Somerset), on to Ford Abbey, then back to White Lackington and on to a 'junket' in Hinton Park near Crewkerne. Thence he went to Colyton in east Devon, to the Great House, the home of the Yonges, to Mr. Duke's house in Otterton, and finally to Exeter. It must have been at this time that Monmouth visited Topsham, where at some later date there was still enough enthusiasm for Monmouth for a street and a public house to be named after him.

At all of these places Monmouth was royally received, and he was perhaps convinced by this that he could count on warm support at a more critical time. He was not entirely wrong. In 1685 the people thronged to him, but the landed gentry largely held back. Of this

113 *The Citadel gateway in Plymouth, begun at Charles II's orders in 1666 after the Civil War. It overlooks the town of Plymouth, a parliamentary stronghold in that war and a thorn in the royalists' side.*

group, only Colonel John Speke of White Lackington House turned out for him. All Monmouth's former hosts, however, came under suspicion or worse. Edmund Prideaux of Ford Abbey was fined £14,500, all of which went to Judge Jeffreys; rebel servants of the Yonges were hanged at their gates at Escot. Thomas Thynne of Longleat was dead by 1685, but William Strode of Barrington was arrested. Sir John Sydenham of Brympton and Mr. Duke of Otterton seem to have remained quite inactive. Sir Walter Yonge turned suspicion aside by insisting on the payment of arrears of rent by his 'rebel' tenants at Colyton. Monmouth needed the support of the Whig gentry. Their reluctance to give it was fatal to his cause. Perhaps they had a clear idea of his limitations, and of the likely outcome of his hazardous adventure—and also of James II's vindictive nature. Most of all, they did not wish to restart the Civil War.

Monmouth's expectation of support was partly the reason for his decision to land at Lyme Regis. It was also partly a matter of strategy. The dissenters in the West, and perhaps many others, knew that he was on the way. Troops of horse had been trained for the great day; the *Red Lion* inn at Taunton and the *Horseshoe* at Bristol were both centres of plotting. Though they had foreknowledge of Monmouth's arrival, the dissenters and their friends kept their mouths tightly shut. James II's government, for all its spies and informers, was taken unawares. Monmouth had ten days to get together a force. Lyme was far enough from London to give such a breathing-space, and close to Taunton, the most rebellious and dangerous town in the country in the government's view. There they still celebrated 11 May annually, as the day on which the siege of the town by the royalists during the Civil War had been lifted.

114 *John Flavel, a Congregationalist dissenter.*

The course of Monmouth's subsequent march is well known; from Lyme through Axminster and Chard to Taunton; the proclamation as king in the market-place there; the presentation of the colours by schoolgirls. Then the ominous failure outside Bristol, the skirmish in Keynsham, and the affray at Norton St Philip; followed by the now desperate return to Bridgwater, hemmed in by the Lords Churchill and Feversham to the east with the royal army, and by the Devon militia, led by Lord Albemarle, Monck's son, to the west. Word of a great army of 'clubmen' that was to join him proved to be an illusion. Then followed the night attack by Monmouth's men at Sedgemoor that so nearly came off, had it not been for the fatal and unexpected obstacle of the Bussex Rhine, a deep ditch unseen in the darkness, and the final disaster and confusion of a night battle, and finally the massacre of those who could not escape.

Many Devonians must have been in that battle. The names and numbers of those who joined Monmouth are known; 730 Devonians were rebels. Most of them came from east Devon, close to the line of Monmouth's march: 88 from Colyton and 79 from Axminster; 53 from Honiton; 32 from both Upottery and Luppitt, and others from Stockland Musbury, Tiverton and Sidmouth. Many more might have joined, but the Devon militia, although quite incapable of stopping Monmouth at Axminster, and dubiously loyal, did make it difficult for recruits from the rest of Devon to get through to the Axe valley.

Eighteen Devonshire men were wounded at Sedgemoor, and many more may have been killed. Nine were killed elsewhere, and seven died in prison. Fifty-six were executed, 148 transported and sold as slaves in the West Indies, 40 lost all their lands, and 72 were pardoned. Many more took to the hills, woods or moorlands, and hid from authority until a general pardon was proclaimed in 1686, precariously supported in secret by their families and always liable to betrayal. It must have been a fearful winter for those on the run.

115 *James, Duke of Monmouth.*

These men risked a horrible death on the gallows and ruination for their families by following Monmouth. They were well aware of the dangers; they were not ignorant young labourers seeking excitement. Most of them were dissenters; a great many of the villages whence they came

116 *Escot pillar, where it is said Monmouth rebels were hanged in 1685. Originally at Fairmile, it was flattened by a falling tree and has been rebuilt at Escot lodge gates.*

had dissenting congregations. Many ministers, like Sampson Larke of Combe Raleigh and John Hicks of Kingsbridge, marched with Monmouth. A few were lawyers, like Mathew Bragg of Thorncombe, or surgeons, like Sam Potts of Honiton or Nicholas Thompson of Colyton. Some were landowners in a small way, like Roger Satchell of Colyton, the leader of Monmouth's party there: Colyton was perhaps the most rebellious place apart from Taunton. Most were tradesmen or craftsmen, and a great many were cloth-workers, and in 1685 there was much unemployment and depression in that industry. In Colyton, Taunton and Lyme, over half were mature men in their 30s, probably with wives and families; three-quarters were over twenty-five. A few were in their 50s, old Cromwellian soldiers fighting for 'the good old cause'.

Of all the rebels, it could probably be said as of Cromwell's Ironsides, 'they knew what they were fighting for and loved what they knew'. They looked for freedom to worship as they wished, without persecution; the end of arbitrary government; an end to their fear of a return to popery; and perhaps a return to the civil rights and liberties which they had enjoyed under Cromwell. Perhaps at the back of some minds was the concept of a more equitable society, in which birth and wealth and privilege would not be all-powerful. Some would even have been republicans, wanting no king, but prepared to accept Monmouth for the time being. Above all, however, it was freedom from persecution that they wanted. John Whiting, the Quaker, thought there would have been no rebellion 'if liberty of conscience had been granted'. They did not rebel without thought. It has been shown that often only one member of a family joined Monmouth; others remained uninvolved, perhaps to keep family and property together.

The rebellion was a total and disastrous failure, and it was savagely and brutally suppressed. Judge Jeffreys and the Bloody Assize have left a fearful impression in the West Country. There are still 'Jeffreys Houses' where he stayed, and tradition still points to where rebels' quartered bodies were hung up, for all to see and learn a lesson from. Surgeon Yonge of Plymouth recorded how he encountered heads and quarters 'at all the little towns and bridges and crossways'. Another wrote that 'the stench was so great that the ways were not to be travelled'.

In Devon, 13 rebels were executed, at Colyton, Axminster, Crediton, Exeter, Honiton and Ottery St Mary, and their quarters were displayed all over the county. Twelve suffered at Lyme and 19 at Taunton. All the rebels named in this account were so executed, often before the eyes of their friends and neighbours.

Monmouth's own death was gentler, though brutal enough. His executioner was a bungler, who could not sever his victim's neck with a single stroke of the axe. Monmouth and his cause, though defeated, were not forgotten in the west. Macaulay says that West-Country people, seeking an advocate on a parliamentary matter, felt entitled to seek the help of the Duke of Buccleuch, as Monmouth's direct descendant. It was said that those who helped to defeat Monmouth never prospered. Tom 'Boilman', who boiled the quarters of rebels at Taunton, was killed by a stroke of lightning. Farmer 'Burnguts' Raphael of Combpyne 'visibly pined away', and Anne Farrant, who revealed Monmouth's last hiding-place near Wimborne, ended her life 'in misery'.

The summer of 1686 saw James II on a progress through the West, where he was surprisingly well received. A general pardon had been issued in March, and his later Declaration of Indulgence, granting freedom of worship, disarmed the dissenters to some extent. Briefly these actions gave the King a measure of popular support, but in the next two years his autocratic pro-Catholic policy contrived to create such opposition that in 1688 the West was in arms again.

William of Orange, the protestant champion, at once both James's nephew and son-in-law, landed at Brixham on 5 November. The date was an accidental but fortunate reminder of previous threats to English liberties. The place was almost certainly by choice, though Yorkshire, also well away from London, was considered. In the event the 'Protestant wind' blew William's fleet westwards, and veered to the south just in time to blow him into Torbay. He was carried ashore by a fisherman and well received by local people. One of his first acts was to send a detachment to protestant Lyme, but for a week few supported him, the gentry seemingly unprepared, and the people fearing a repetition of the Bloody Assize. William stayed at Ford House in Newton Abbot—the bed he slept in still survives—where his Declaration was read, and he made a grand and triumphant entry into Exeter, and took up residence at the Deanery, although Bishop Lamplugh fled the city.

117 *Statue of William of Orange, William III, at Brixham. He landed there on 5 November 1688, carried ashore by a fisherman, on his way to take the throne from James II.*

118 *Scythe blades used as weapons by rebels.*

Eventually, as James hesitated (immobilised for a time by a disastrous nose-bleed) the tide began to turn William's way. Lord Cornbury, James's brother-in-law, the son of the Earl of Clarendon who had been Charles II's senior statesman, brought his unsuspecting regiment to Honiton and offered his services. That perhaps was the turning-point. Sir Edward Seymour of Berry Pomeroy rode in, and Sir John Grenville, the Earl of Bath, in command of the Plymouth garrison, also declared for William. Men who had opposed and defeated Monmouth on James's behalf now deserted him for William. Amongst them was John Churchill, later to be Duke of Marlborough. Encouraged by this growing support, William rode to Axminster, where he spent several days, and from there he progressed by stages to London, whence James had fortunately fled. There were skirmishes with James's troops at Wincanton and Reading, but no actual battles. London welcomed William. Parliamentary government and the protestant religion were now safe, and toleration was the order of the day.

William's successful 'Glorious Revolution', better planned, organised and equipped, and ultimately well-supported, vindicated Monmouth's aims and to some extent redeemed his failure. After 1688 it might have been expected that Monmouth would have become a Whig hero and martyr. But amongst his followers, as we have seen, were republicans and 'levellers' with radical ideas about society and government which alarmed the property-owning constitutional Whig elite. Having won their contest with the crown, they had no intention of remodelling society or sharing power with the mass of the people. Monmouth was never rehabilitated, though his followers were pardoned and his descendants eventually ennobled.

By 1688, 46 years had passed since swords were first drawn in the west in conflict; doubtless in many minds there were memories of tales of earlier commotions in 1549 and 1497. Two perilous, passionate and strenuous centuries had passed. Life in Devon in the future was to be safer, but much less eventful. Monmouth's rising was the last English rebellion, and also the last occasion on which Devonshire people were directly involved in deciding national history.

119   *Playing cards from the Monmouth rebellion.*

15

The Eighteenth Century

After 1688 the political and religious turmoil that had riven the county subsided. The Bloody Assize had made the consequences of rebellion ferociously clear, and there was little support for the Stuart cause in the county in 1715 and 1745. Toleration was now law, so the old religious disputes between the established church and the dissenters gave way to grudging co-existence. Elsewhere in the country, political disputes gave way in importance to industrial and economic change in the form of the Industrial Revolution. Devon, however, escaped this great upheaval: there was no coal, its industries were well-established, traditional, and largely in the hands of a merchant oligarchy. Reluctance to change and to re-invest ensured that changes which transformed industry elsewhere passed Devon by. By the end of the 18th century both cloth-making and mining were in decline, though there were pockets of survival. On the borders of Cornwall, and here and there elsewhere in Devon, miners were still at work. In the Culm valley the Fox family kept cloth-making going, and it survived in a few other places, notably Ashburton, largely for political reasons.

120 *Hourglass stand, from Ashton Church pulpit.*

Trade too was in decline, and the 18th century saw the virtual end of Exeter as a port and manufacturing centre. Significantly, the Baring family left Exeter for London to found their banking house. All that survives of them in Exeter is one small street that bears their name. Other merchant families, like the Kennaways and the Cholwiches, the Northcotes and the Davys, forsook trade and joined the ranks of the landed gentry. Exeter, by the end of the century, was thus largely a service town; a cathedral city, a county capital. Its mercantile and manufacturing heyday was now in the past.

It was the same story in many other Devon towns, their trade hit by the constant French wars and the loss of the American colonies. There were exceptions; Plymouth's history became increasingly bound up with the navy. Its dockyard helped to service the fleet that blockaded the French ports during the great struggles with France. Elsewhere, Sidmouth, Dawlish and Exmouth were beginning to develop as resorts. But the centre of gravity of industry, and the trade that went with it, had passed to the north of England. Devon was no longer one of the richer English counties, as the new wealth was measured.

For the ordinary man and woman, perhaps the most significant thing was that the population of the county nearly doubled. This, combined with slowly declining trade and industry, meant unemployment and low wages. Labourers' wages hardly grew in the century, though the cost of living probably increased by half. More and more of the poor were thrown on the parish. A look at any parish's poor book reveals the same story—poor rates rising, numbers on relief rising, the word 'pauper' being used for the first time in some parishes.

Worse was to come when the wars against revolutionary France broke out. Dartmouth, Brixham, Exeter, Totnes and some rural areas all rioted against the millers and farmers who, it was said, kept the price of wheat high by exporting or hoarding. To the alarm of the authorities, in Brixham and Dartmouth the militia joined the rioters. These militiamen were local folk, part-time soldiers, recruited to ward off a French invasion force. The authorities viewed the situation as an extremely grave one, and the rioters were harshly dealt with. The name of Thomas Campion of Ilsington, who was hanged at Bovey Heathfield in 1795 for his part in the riot at Bellamarsh Mill, and who was escorted to his execution by 'a thousand military', is still remembered. Five other men were hanged at Stonegallows, just over the Somerset border near Wellington, in 1801. Earlier in the century there had been food riots in Exeter in 1761, and in Ottery St Mary in 1766; and strikes amongst the cloth-workers of Exeter and Tiverton and in the Culm valley.

121 *Jolly Lane Cottage, Hexworthy, was originally a squatters' cottage built on common land with a chimney smoking in 24 hours, as 'squatters' rights' demanded.*

Devon did not suffer from the enclosure movement as did other areas, for its fields had largely been enclosed for centuries. Common land provided opportunities for squatters, and this was a way up the economic ladder for a few, but it is likely that the typical English rural social pattern of farmer and farm labourer (in contrast with a land-holding peasantry) had established itself in Devon by this time. The Hemyock parish registers, already cited, provide evidence of this tendency. The commons, where the poor often had grazing and wood-gathering rights, first began to be enclosed during the French wars, as every acre that would grow corn was needed. Much of the tops of the Blackdown Hills in east Devon and elsewhere were enclosed by parliamentary acts, at the behest of the landowning class. Doubtless more food was produced, but the poor man's 'squatter's rights' thus tended to disappear. Enclosure landscape from this period—largish rectangular surveyed fields, straight roads with wide verges—is not uncommon in east Devon.

XII *Appledore's covered shipyard dates from 1971 and is capable of building ships up to 10,000 tons. It is the only yard building merchant ships still at work in England.*

XIII *Roadford Reservoir was finished in 1989 and supplies the needs of Plymouth and North Devon. Farmhouses were flooded to create this resource.*

XIV *The Tamar bridges. Brunel's railway bridge was built in 1859. The new Tamar bridge is the only road bridge crossing of the river below the medieval 'New' bridge at Gunnislake, at least 10 miles upstream.*

The gentry continued to dominate Devonshire society in this century and for some time thereafter, as elsewhere. They had won their struggle with the monarchy. Now they ran their own 'countries', as they called them, more or less as they pleased. They were the M.P.s and the justices of the peace; they administered the poor law through the overseers they appointed; they fixed the maximum wages. Much of the land was theirs, many farmers were their tenants. They had enormous power, which they might or might not use benevolently. No area of Devon was exempt from their control, though many villages had no resident squire or great house.

122 *The elegant lodgings at Fortfield Terrace, Sidmouth, which were begun in 1792. Sidmouth was a popular resort for the well-to-do from the late 18th century, made more so by the Duke of Kent, Queen Victoria's father.*

The origins of the landowning class were various. Some, like the Aclands and the Cholwiches, had ancestors who were freeholders in medieval times, who had hung on to and added to their estates by judicious marriages and hard work. The fortunes of others, like the Rolles, Wadhams, Fortescues and Prideaux, were based on the law; Devon abounded with lawyers. Some had bought monastic estates cheaply. Some, like the Yonges of Escot, the Kennaways, the Willoughbys of Leyhill, and the Davies of Creedy Park, were merchants who had bought their way into landed society. A few—the Kellys of Kelly, the Fursdons of Fursdon, and the Fulfords of Fulford, for instance—lived, and still live, on the estates which their ancestors had owned or leased since not long after the Norman Conquest. None (except perhaps the Pomeroys, the earls of Harberton) could justly claim to have come over with the Conqueror. Parish churches are full of memorials to this much-interrelated ruling class.

The gentry built themselves fine houses, and surrounded them with parks. Very few in Devon—perhaps only Saltram in Plympton, Castle Hill in Filleigh, and Powderham—can be called 'great houses' in the manner of Hatfield or Burleigh. Most Devonshire houses bear a close relationship to the comparatively small estates of Devonshire gentry. Some, like Bearescombe and Keynedon near Kingsbridge, were enlarged Tudor or medieval farmhouses. Others, like Fulford, Bovey House at Beer, or what are now the melancholy ruins of Fowellscombe near Ugborough, were small Tudor mansions. Some few, like Compton Castle and Bradley Manor, are late medieval, as is Dartington, on a grander scale. Some, like Puslinch, Mothecombe or Withycombe House, Stokenham, are 18th-century.

Hunting, shooting, fishing, preserving game, entertaining their friends, managing their estates and sitting on the Bench were the principal occupations of the gentry. Combe near Gittisham, built by the Putts about 1600, and still owned by their descendants the Markers, is a fine

123-27 *Kelly House in the parish of Kelly* (left), *Great Fulford in Dunsford* (middle left), *Fursdon in Cadbury* (middle right), *Seccombe in Germansweek* (bottom left) *and Reddaway in Sampford Courtenay* (bottom right). *These are owned to this day by the Kellys, Fulfords, Fursdons, Seccombes and Reddaways who took their names from their property and have all been there for upwards of 750 years—in the case of the Kellys probably since the Conquest.*

example of a squire's house, with its hall, its walled garden, its ha-ha, its lake, landscaped park and fine 'prospects'. Here gentry kept some state and entertained their neighbours amongst fine furniture and fittings. Others lived in the old rough way, untouched by elegant 18th-century manners. Squire Arscott of Tetcott kept a jester, Black John, who 'mumbled' sparrows, rolling them over in his mouth until all the feathers were gone, or swallowed live mice (tied securely by a string) for the entertainment of his master's guests. The gentry exerted a great deal of influence through the established church. Most anglican clergymen came from gentry families. The squire would have his special pew in church, whence he could observe the congregation, itself arranged in order of precedence. Observing them also were the parson and the parish clerk, from one of the great three-decker pulpits so common in the 18th century. The combination of parson and squire, drawn from the same class, could be formidable, and there was truth in the saying that the anglican church was 'the Tory party at prayer'.

The church in the diocese as a whole, as in much of England, was hardly notable for its enthusiasm or efficiency. There was a good deal of absenteeism and pluralism amongst the clergy, but the latter was almost inescapable when stipends in some parishes amounted to hardly more than a labourer's wage. There were surprisingly few 'scandalous clerks', but tithes were still, as in previous centuries, a great source of dispute between clergy and laity. The church showed an interest in education and in the care of the sick, and kept a hold of a sort over morality through its ecclesiastical courts. It seems to have made little provision for the emotional and spiritual needs of its flock.

These were met in part by Methodism. John Wesley made 30 preaching tours through Devon, although Cornwall was always more fruitful ground for him. By the end of the century there were four methodist 'circuits' or linked groups of chapels in Devon, with 1,300 members. A little later methodists were recorded in 150 different Devon parishes. Methodism, like the older forms of dissent, offered a chance for ordinary people to express themselves away from the control of the establishment, and thus acquired—although this was far from Wesley's original intentions—certain political overtones. Dissenting chapels could sometimes provide meeting-places for workers considering united action against low wages or harsh conditions, and lay preaching trained many in the techniques of public speaking which could be turned to secular use. Early in the 18th century there were still at least 85 meeting houses in the county, and perhaps one in five of the county's population was a dissenter, a member of a presbyterian or congregationalist meeting. Enthusiasm

128 *Black John, the four-foot hunchbacked fool of Squire Arscott of Tetcott in north Devon. He followed the hounds on foot, mumbled the feathers off living sparrows with his lips, and swallowed and retrieved live mice tied to a string for the entertainment of his master's guests. He died in 1788, a relic from past ages still acceptable in backward rustic Devon.*

129 *Parracombe old church. This has an almost perfect unmodernised 18th-century interior. The church was abandoned in 1878 but has been preserved.*

for these sects declined with the century. The presbyterian church was split country-wide by a controversy (which began in Exeter) over the Trinity, and within Devon many of its most influential supporters—well-to-do cloth merchants and skilled artisans—fell away as cloth-making declined.

For many of the gentry the most rewarding activity was politics. In Devon, as in England as a whole, there were at that time no major political or religious issues to divide the country. Politics had resolved itself into a power struggle, a game in which the financial, and less tangible, rewards were considerable. The gentry contested these in Devon's 12 borough and two county seats; there were 26 parliamentary seats for the county in all. The dukes of Bedford controlled two of them—Okehampton and Tavistock—by patronage, and through their tenants. Dartmouth was the 'property' of the Holdsworths, the Newmans and the Seales. Ashburton always sent Jardines and Mathesons to parliament, and in return these two East India Company families kept Ashburton cloth-making going.

The electorate was limited in most of the boroughs to the corporation and the freemen, and these were usually nominees of the controlling gentry family. Tiverton had only 24 voters. Honiton had the largest electorate—about five hundred of them—who had either votes by 'scot and lot' (i.e. they were ratepayers), or were 'potwallopers' (householders). The Yonges of Escot controlled one Honiton seat until it bankrupted them (it is said to have cost them £240,000). The Courtenays and the Poles controlled the other for a long time. From about 1760, because of its large electorate, Honiton attracted the radical politicians of the day. Alderman Brass Crosby, a friend of Wilkes, Cobbett and Lord Cochrane all stood for Honiton. It was an immensely expensive procedure, costing candidates as much as £8 a vote at a time when £16 was more than a half-a-year's wages for a labourer. Each voter had two votes to bestow. Cobbett claimed that Honiton lived by its votes. There were 16 firms of lawyers in the town and elections of one sort or another were held in the town roughly every three years. The polls stayed open a week and voters waited to see who would pay them most. To help win support, pubs stayed open 24 hours a day, and drinks were free; there were processions, demonstrations and even battles. Such was 18th-century politics in Honiton, perhaps worse than most, but not untypical, except insofar as it elected radicals, whereas most M.P.s were strictly of and for the 'establishment'.

130 *Three-decker pulpit, Parracombe old church.*

By the end of the century towns had begun to 'improve' themselves, knocking down old-fashioned market houses, widening and paving the roads, and installing street lighting and water supplies. Where it could be afforded, slate took the place of the dangerous thatch as a roofing material. In east Devon there were no cheap local supplies of slate, and all the towns there suffered a number of disastrous fires, one of the last (at Ottery St Mary) taking place in 1866. Because of these fires, few pre-18th-century buildings appear to survive in these towns. Ottery, Honiton, Cullompton and Tiverton had all been 'cloth' towns; with the decline of the industry they were less prosperous. The cost of repairing the fire damage, even with the help in some cases of fire insurance payments, merely compounded the problem. Elsewhere in Devon (with the notable exceptions of Chudleigh and Moreton-hampstead), fires seem to have been less frequent.

Some towns, like South Molton and Torrington, were prosperous enough to build elegant town halls. Many too had their own local banks, sometimes precariously funded. Devon was at last responding to the new economy, but its own was in decline. The new turnpikes, making possible vastly increased coach traffic into the county, and the emergence of Sidmouth and Exmouth as fashionable resorts, pointed the way to the county's future.

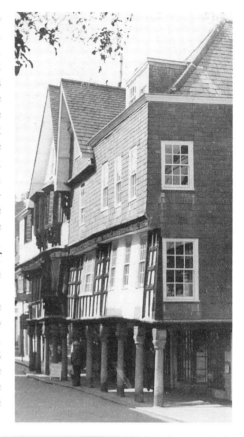

131 Above right. *The Butterwalk, Dartmouth, built c.1640. The arcading could protect market 'perishables' from the weather, and made an extra room above.*

132 Right. *The Guildhall at Totnes, the seat of town government. It was built c.1553 on part of the site of Totnes Priory.*

16

The Nineteenth Century

An intelligent and observant traveller visiting Devon towards the middle of the 18th century would have seen much on which to comment. He would have found the hedged, enclosed, pastoral landscape unusual and interesting, and even beautiful. He would have noted the many busy towns, each with its market, its merchants' houses, and its many courts and alleys, where the almost ubiquitous trade of making cloth was carried on; and the populous villages where a productive and efficient use of the land was combined with industry, spinning and weaving, lace-making, tanning, and paper-making.

If he had passed over the wastes of Dartmoor, he might have seen a few tinners at work, and noticed signs of much greater past activity. By the sea, he would have remarked on the Royal Dockyard at what was to become Devonport, and on the shipping clustered in every Devon harbour, and the fishing-boats drawn up on every beach. He would have

133 *Turnpike roads.*

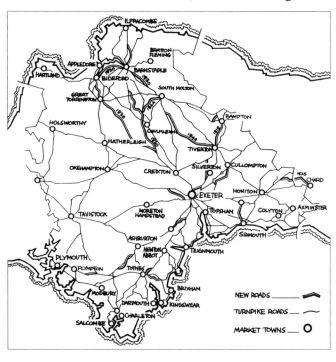

noticed a number of substantial manor-houses, and gentlemen's seats, but remarked, perhaps, on the absence of all but a few 'great' houses. If he had gone to matins on a Sunday morning he might have commented on the church's old-fashioned furniture and fittings, and perhaps indeed on its old-fashioned parson. Where they had not been rebuilt after a fire, he would have found the thatch and cob of the towns and villages also reminiscent of a past age.

He would have met much good company in the inns; many rich merchants and well-to-do squires; and a visit to market would have introduced him to a tolerably prosperous class of yeomen farmers, and rather poorer but not backward husbandmen. In contrast, a chance-met tinner or cloth-worker might have impressed him by his industry, but also by his poverty.

118

Such a traveller, at the end of the next century, would perhaps have remarked on busy industrious Plymouth, and on the holiday towns popular with the middle classes, but would have found Devon old-fashioned, bucolic and behind the times, a county that had been by-passed by great industrial and economic changes. But of course Devon was not unchanged by the Industrial Revolution and all that went with it. Railways and better roads ensured that the county was far more closely linked with the rest of the country, and that its old economic and cultural isolation was to some extent lost.

There had been other great changes. As with the rest of the country, the population had vastly increased, nearly doubling from 340,000 to 660,000 between 1801 and 1901. Elsewhere in England, mills, coal mines, factories, foundries and shipyards absorbed much of this extra population. But Devon had no coal for steam power and, in particular, none for the making of iron and steel on any scale. Heavy industry established itself most readily where coal and iron ore were close at hand and cheap. Devon's considerable supplies of minerals almost invariably had to be exported for processing.

There was in fact water enough to power many factories, and here and there, at Ottery, Tiverton, and in the Culm valley, it was so used, but ultimately the economic advantage lay elsewhere, and so the material results of the Industrial Revolution—factory towns, slum housing, blast furnaces and coal pits—are almost entirely absent from the county. Most villages and towns declined in prosperity, size, and consequence, and the wages for those who chose not to leave were pitifully low. Devon experienced 'de-industrialisation', not unlike what has been diagnosed in the whole country today. 'Services' are the prescribed substitute for industry today. In Devon tourism, and domestic, administrative, and retailing services, largely replaced industry, except in Plymouth and in a few towns favoured by local circumstances.

Industry died slowly in Devon, and its decline was by no means uniform. By 1851 Exeter's famous cloth trade employed only 126 workers, and had been largely dead since 1815. There were still 39 spinning mills at work in the county in 1838, but only 20 by 1850. At that date there were still 3,300 looms at work, but these were all handlooms, and handloom weaving was so badly paid that most of the paupers 'relieved' in Crediton at that time were weavers. Spinning lingered here and there until the end of the century and after; in the Culm valley, for instance, Fox Brothers were to make army puttees well into the 20th century, and at Bideford labour-intensive collar making was introduced, and Torrington made high-quality gloves. At Axminster, Thomas Whitty's carpet-making survived until the 1830s, when the business was transferred to Wilton. Around Honiton, lace continued until the First World War to be made on a diminishing scale by poorly-paid hand workers. There were occasional flurries of activity stimulated by fashion or royal patronage, but the trade was hit by the introduction of machine net made, notably, at Tiverton by Thomas Heathcote.

134 *The carpet factory at Axminster was begun by Thomas Whitty in 1755 but failed in 1835. It was successfully revived after 1945 by Harry Dutfield.*

135 *The quay at Morwellham from which 'half the world's' copper supply was exported in the mid-19th century from Great Consols mine five miles upstream, then the property of the Duke of Bedford. The dock was dug out and rescued from dereliction after 1970.*

Mining followed rather a different pattern. There was a brief revival after the mid-century; 4,000 miners were at work in 1881, compared with half that figure in 1841, but by 1900 there was little left of a once-thriving industry. Dartmoor tin was largely worked out, though some 66 mines, many probably very small-scale enterprises, can be counted at work at different dates over the last half-century. Vitifer Mine near the Warren House, one of the biggest, produced 154 tons in 1864, but only 22 tons in 1907, with a workforce, then, of thirty-five. Devon produced on average less than one per cent of the national total of tin.

In contrast, copper, silver, lead and manganese mines were far more productive. New silver and lead mines were opened in the Teign and Tamar valleys and at Combe Martin, which produced between them five per cent of the country's lead, and at one time 20 per cent of its silver, this last mainly from the Tamar mines. Wheal Exmouth at Christow, and Tamar Silver at Bere Ferrers, were two of the biggest of the 48 silver/lead mines. Manganese deposits were discovered at Upton Pyne, Newton St Cyres, Milton Abbot and Marystow, north of Tavistock. Between 1850 and 1876 Devon's mines produced 90 per cent of the country's output of this material, so vital for steelmaking. For a time Devon had been the only supplier of the ore in Europe. Chillaton Mine at Milton Abbot was the biggest of Devon's 25 mines.

But by far the most spectacular success was in copper mining. Devon Great Consols, above the Tamar between Gunnislake and Tavistock, epitomised the dreams of many mining speculators, and made many fortunes. Its total production was 750,000 tons of high-grade copper, and for a time it was the largest copper mine in the world, employing a workforce of 1,200. When copper declined in price, it turned to arsenic, producing in 1869 half the world's output. The Duke of Bedford, on whose land it stood, drew royalties of £270,000 over 30 years. The mines of the Tamar valley, the inclined planes, water-wheels, chimneys, flues and furnaces, the mineral port of Morwellham and the Tavistock canal are monuments to 19th-century industrial enterprise. Arsenic and fluorspar from the Tamar mines, barytes from the Teign valley, zinc from around Ilsington, were all secondary products of Devon mines. Almost all the country's fluorspar, used in the making of iron, at one time came from Devon. Iron was mined at North Molton, Molland, around Bovey Tracey, and at Brixham. Welsh steel makers took an interest in the Exmoor mines—one was named Cwm Molton.

In all there were perhaps two to three hundred mines at work at different dates in the county, employing perhaps at most 5,000-6,000 men, only a tiny proportion of the county's workforce, but stimulating much other work and producing wealth probably well out of proportion to the numbers employed. Unlike Devon Great Consols, many of the mines were probably small-scale, primitive enterprises, employing a few semi-independent workers. Landowners like the Bampfyldes at North Molton and the Pellews of the Teign valley probably drew considerable royalties, if not on the scale of the Duke of Bedford.

In contrast, wages for miners were low, perhaps 14 shillings a week in the 1860s, but almost inevitably they were higher than farmworkers' wages, so there was always a ready supply of labour. Disputes seem to have been few, since the miners normally negotiated their own piecework rates, and even on occasion took a share in the ore they raised. At Devon Great Consols there was an alarming strike in 1866, when troops were brought in, special constables recruited, blacklegs attacked and their attackers jailed. But there were too many unemployed miners for the strike to succeed, and the union the miners tried to form disintegrated. Its members were all sacked.

With declining numbers in textiles, and few employed in mining, farming absorbed nearly one man in four of the working population. During the period of high prices in the French wars, farming had prospered inordinately. Wages, subsidised out of the poor rate, in no way kept up with prices, and farmers and millers became immensely unpopular, inspiring riots in the towns, the occasional attack on a mill and forced sales of corn at a 'fair' price. Land that had not felt the plough for centuries grew corn profitably.

136 *Whitworks tin mine, Dartmoor.*

But this level of prosperity did not outlast the end of the wars in 1815. Farm rents, a good indicator of prosperity, more than doubled on Lord Sidmouth's estates at Upottery in the war years, fell by a quarter by 1820, but were back to near war levels by 1827, by which time Upottery farmers had reverted to the pastoral farming that they did best. Despite the repeal of the Corn Laws—the protective duty on corn—in 1846, farmers continued to prosper.

There were technical improvements. The bigger, corn-selling farms installed water, or horse-driven threshing machines: mangolds were introduced, and the proper growing of turnips encouraged, but observers found farmers reluctant to change their ways. Societies were formed, however, for the two much-admired Devon cattle breeds: the six Devon sheep breeds were becoming recognisable; and local 'improvement societies' were widely formed. Yields of corn improved, and average farm size increased. By the end of the century, there were 54 farm implement makers and dealers in the county, selling seed drills, reapers and sowing-machines, as well as improved ploughs, some of local design like the Huxtable.

Nevertheless, there were still 'heretic' farmers, who 'burnt beat' and scorned 'boughten' feeding stuffs, who grew little corn for sale. In the event, the heretics survived rather better than the 'orthodox' when the great agricultural depression bankrupted great numbers of 'up-country' farmers. After the 1870s cheap imported American and Canadian corn caused a disastrous fall in prices, but in Devon it was easy (and customary) to revert to grass. Just over half the land was under grass in 1855, but

137 *The railway network.*

by 1901 the proportion was nearly three-quarters. Farm rents on Lord Sidmouth's estates fell by only 12 per cent compared with 40 per cent falls in the arable counties. At the turn of the century there were no farms unlet in Devon on Lord Fortescue's estates, and only one per cent of his tenants were behind with the rent.

Cattle, pig and sheep numbers increased by roughly a third; butter made from scalded cream was exported in quantity. The resultant whey fed many pigs, notably in east Devon, where at Hemyock, at the head of a branch railway line, a well-known pig market was established that sent many 'porkers' to London. The numbers of cattle sent out of the county by railway trebled between 1850 and 1910, thus creating vastly greater markets than in the old 'droving' days when far fewer cattle went not much further than Bristol. Markets were set up near the railway, at Halwill and Sidmouth junctions, for instance. At Hemyock the railway stimulated four local farmers to set up a creamery to market their own and their neighbours' butter, and much the same was done at Torrington.

Some favoured areas were enabled by the railways to cash in on horticulture. Strawberry growing flourished in the Tamar valley from the 1870s, supplementing the already abundant cherries. Later, narcissi were introduced for the London market. Dawlish grew 'Devon violets'; Combe Martin grew strawberries for Ilfracombe; Newton Poppleford, early peas; and Alphington, gooseberries.

Such prosperity as there was did not filter through to the farm labourer until the last two decades of the century. In the 1860s when farm rents were at their highest, Devon farm workers' wages were only three-quarters of the penurious national wage. Labourers were appallingly housed, worse educated and partly stupefied by abundant 'free' cider, which in fact formed part of their wages. It was these conditions which prompted Canon Girdlestone, vicar of Halberton near Tiverton, to harangue the farmers from his pulpit and in the press, and to organise the movement of labourers to better-paid jobs in the north and overseas. He was horrified at the apathy of this 'beaten' class, but even he was reluctant to support the formation of a branch of Joseph Arch's farmworkers' union.

The response of Devon country folk to their miserable conditions was to leave. Village populations reached their peak around 1850, wages their lowest level relatively in the 1860s. Between 1851 and 1901, some 371,000 folk, more or less the total population of the county in 1801, left

Devon to find work elsewhere. Of these, 126,000 left England altogether. The population of most inland villages was halved. A village of 500 souls might have seen 350 leave in 60 years. These migration figures are higher than for other English rural areas, and higher even than the figures for southern Ireland between 1860 and 1880, after the famine. Economically, perhaps, this migration was desirable; there was a need for labour elsewhere; but the human cost was immense. Of those who stayed, many were old and infirm, and the workhouses of Devon, the hated 'Bastilles', had relatively more 'aged and impotent' residents than in other parts of the country.

In contrast, some parts of the county, and some towns, grew during this period. Plymouth's population grew from 43,000 in 1801 to 186,000 in 1901. By the latter date nearly a third of the population of Devon lived in Plymouth; in 1801 it had been one-seventh. In 1911 two-thirds of the population lived in a few growing towns, or along the coast; in 1801 the figure had been one-third. No less than 156,000 folk moved into Devon between 1850 and 1900, almost entirely to these growing towns, and particularly to Plymouth.

After the migration from the villages, there were no longer unemployed labourers hanging about them in hope of work. Farmworkers' wages rose after 1870, until in 1907 they were very close to the national figure. In contrast, in the corn-growing counties, wages fell after 1870. Prices remained more or less static, so the standard of living rose. But farm work was still the worst-paid of all occupations, and the workers' tied houses were often rural slums. Urban wages, even for craftsmen, never caught up with the national average before the First World War, and in 1913 the Devon wage for all jobs was only three-quarters of the national figure.

In mid-century, with rising prices, low wages had caused real distress in the towns. In Exeter in 1847, 1854 and 1867, there were bread riots; the city was prone to mob violence, and ineffectively policed. Anti-Popish riots marked many Guy Fawkes days, and low church emotions were roused to riot when Anglican clergy were ordered to wear surplices. Exeter people, many living in the insanitary slums where cholera hit hard, hated the police and the yeomanry, who put down these troubles with difficulty.

Other towns shared in this distress, but Plymouth was the great exception. It was a 'boom' town, the only place in the county that was in any real sense industrialised. Although it was described as the next most insanitary town in Europe after Warsaw, at least wages were far higher than in the rest of the county. Much government money was pumped into the dockyard; there were breweries, distilleries, a starch factory, soap and paint makers. It was by far the biggest port in the county, taking two-thirds of the local, and three-quarters of the foreign trade. It was, from the 1870s, a great liner port; at its height, some 500 liners visited Plymouth in a year, their passengers being ferried ashore by specially-built tenders.

138 Below left. *The Normandie rounding Plymouth break-water in 1935, after the fastest crossing of the Atlantic. She is flying the Blue Riband.*

139 Below right. *Brunel's 'Atmospheric' line broken by the sea between Dawlish and Teignmouth.*

140 Middle. *Storm bound shipping in Plymouth Sound.*

141 Bottom. *The Channel Fleet in Plymouth Sound.*

Elsewhere in the county, Teignmouth profited from the increasing exports of ball clay from the Bovey basin; Peters Marland clay in north Devon was also worked extensively. Newton Abbot became something of a railway town, and at Barnstaple Brannams made high-quality pottery, and Shaplands pioneered the movement towards mass-produced furniture. At Exeter and Hele, amongst many other places, there were paper mills, and Exeter also had iron foundries, one of which made the 'Bodley' cooking stove, beloved of Devon farmers' wives. Ship-building and repairing flourished at Appledore and Dartmouth, but the yards and the ports, Plymouth apart, could hardly cope with the new, much larger, ships.

The export of Devonshire cattle, sheep and pigs, Devonshire straw-berries and butter, and the migration of Devon people, was made much easier by the coming of the railways. The railway reached Exeter from Bristol in 1844, and within a decade Plymouth and Barnstaple were linked; within 35 years the whole county was provided with quick, cheap transport. In 1837 it cost 18 shillings to travel from Bideford to Exeter

by road; in 1850 Exeter to Birmingham by rail was 14 shillings. Where ordinary folk once walked, or took the unhurried carriers' cart, now they could ride at what was then a frightening speed. In this way the county's former isolation was broken down.

The broad-gauge Great Western, and the standard-gauge Southern railways now connected Devon to the rest of England. Brunel built his adventurous but unsuccessful Atmospheric railway from Exeter to Newton Abbot, and his Royal Albert Bridge across the Tamar, to the alarm of the Cornish. Both railways provided useful, well-thought-of jobs for local people, and the G.W.R., 'God's Wonderful Railway', attracted much praise and even affection. But by 1903 more than half Devon's freight tonnage, coal in particular, was still being carried by the hundreds of brigs and schooners, and later tramps, that put into Devon's smaller ports, and the bigger ships that put into Plymouth.

Except in the remotest corners, coach traffic was killed stone-dead, and there was less call for the carriers' carts. The Grand Western Canal fell into decay. Some towns (Ashburton and Chulmleigh for instance) were by-passed by the railways and declined; some, like Kingsbridge, lost their local industry once the railway came. Country folk could now have a day in Exeter or Plymouth to taste city life, but many were content to eschew such 'tripsing and traipsing' and some of the character of village life, so much admired by visitors, remained.

It is unlikely that tourism could ever have developed in the way it did without the railways. Dawlish, Exmouth, Sidmouth and Torbay were already exclusive resorts for the well-to-do, and elegant terraces and villas had been built. Better and, in some cases, new roads had made this

142 Top. *Coburg Terrace, Sidmouth,* c.*1830.*

143 Above. *Part of* Woodland Hotel *in* 'cottage ornée' *style,* c.*1850. Many existing hotels and apartment houses in Sidmouth began life as gentlemen's 'cottages'.*

144 *'The sea side' at Babbacombe beach.*

possible. But the railways opened up Devon to the less well-off. Fares to Ilfracombe were deliberately set high to deter those working people who could afford a holiday; hoteliers there were aghast at the arrival of a shipload of Welsh miners from across the Bristol Channel.

However, the resorts gradually adapted themselves to a new clientèle. Purpose-built terraces of lodging houses or 'rooms' were erected, and assembly rooms, parks and promenades created for the visitors' delectation. Dawlish is credited with the first bathing machines. Devon had 1,000 hotels or lodging houses by 1856, and 3,000 by 1914. Tourists found the red soil and green, pastoral landscape engaging, the air healthy, and a pleasantly cheap and unspoilt county at the end of their railway journey. Elegant prints and views of 'seats' and antiquities were produced at least partly as souvenirs for the visitor. Thackeray, Dickens, Keats and Southey were among the men of letters who visited the county.

The Industrial Revolution had imposed major changes on the economy of Devon. Industry itself was largely a thing of the past; farming still prospered modestly; providing for the visitor was a new source of growth. Politically, control fell even more firmly, if anything, into the hands of the landed classes, despite the three Reform Bills that gave more and more ordinary folk the vote. The pocket and rotten boroughs—Honiton, Ashburton, Okehampton and Bere Ferrers amongst them—were gradually disfranchised. By 1885 the county was divided into four districts and these, with Plymouth, Devonport and Exeter, elected 13 M.P.s compared with the 26 M.P.s elected before 1832.

The towns tended to elect local businessmen, but in the districts the old landed families held almost exclusive sway, and were perhaps better represented than they had been before 1832. The Palks, the Aclands, the Fortescues, the Chichesters and the Russells supplied many M.P.s, voted in by their tenants in often uncontested elections, not just out of deference, but because they best represented 'the land' and farming. Many of these landed members were Liberals, somewhat of the old Whiggish variety, and in many general elections Liberals were in a majority in the county, backed perhaps by a strong nonconformist vote. Lord John Russell, Prime Minister and leader of the Whigs, was M.P. for Tavistock and for South Devon. Lord Palmerston, Prime Minister and Foreign Secretary, represented Tiverton for nearly 30 years. Sir Stafford Northcote, M.P. for North Devon, was Chancellor of the Exchequer in 1874.

The Chartists, the left-wing radicals of their day, made little impact on the county, though Exeter was proposed as one of their 'land settlements', where the urban unemployed might return to the land. George Harney, a noted Chartist leader, stood against Lord Palmerston and Thomas Heathcote in Tiverton. Uniquely perhaps, he got no votes. Henry Vincent, another Chartist, stood for industrial Plymouth and mining Tavistock, and Sam Carter, a local lawyer, was Chartist M.P. for Tavistock briefly in 1852.

The great estate owners, and their tenants, still dominated the scene. Outside Plymouth and Exeter, only Thomas Heathcote, M.P. for Tiverton from 1832 to 1857, came from the new important class of industrialists. In 1874 the Rolles still owned 55,000 acres, the Courtenays and the Fortescues 20,000, Lord Clinton 14,000 and there were in all 190 estates of over 1,000 acres. Only 18 per cent of the land was owner occupied; the great landowners owned a fifth of the county, the gentry nearly a third: but there was still nearly a third in the hands of those owning less than 300 acres.

Perhaps the most significant change was in local government, when the county council was established in 1889 with elected councillors. Previously, affairs had been in the hands of village vestries, and of borough councils in the towns, and those of the magistrates at quarter sessions, all largely self-perpetuating non-elective bodies. Like the local Boards of

145 *Fishing from an open beach at Sidmouth, the town's main livelihood until the end of the 18th century when visitors became important.*

146 *Exmoor sheep.*

Education, of Highways and of Sanitation, they were all dominated by the landowners and the clergy. The village lost control over its own roads, and its poor after 1834 were forced into the local Union Work-houses, often far away from neighbours and relatives, where the regime was deliberately severe.

However, after 1870 every parish had to have its own school, and every Devon child then had at least the chance of literacy. In 1820 perhaps half Devon's villages had a school of some sort, and this number was increased to nearly 400 in 1865 by the building of many church and a few nonconformist schools. Some farmers saw a cheap source of labour disappearing, and there were those who thought the education of the working class politically dangerous. Many labourers needed their children's earnings too much to send them to school regularly.

Anglican instruction, and Anglican domination of the village school, was resented by nonconformists. Education and religion were controversially entwined. In rural north Devon, the Bible Christian sect, led by William O'Bryan and James Thorne, established itself in 1815 at Shebbear and spread from there far afield. Its chapels are a feature in and around many north Devon villages. Plymouth saw the formation in 1830 of the Plymouth Brethren, though the inspiration for this powerful but fissiparous movement was originally from Ireland. The deluded prophetess Joanna Southcott was born at Gittisham. Her belief in the imminence of the Second Coming was shared by thousands, though by few in Devon. Few parts of the county, however, were without a Brethren, a Primitive Methodist, or a Bible Christian chapel. Loyalty to chapel— or church—was a feature of the life of many villagers.

The diocese of Exeter, out of which that of Truro was created in 1878, was not without its controversies. The abrasive, high church, Tory Bishop Philpott, father of 18 children, finally roused the Church in Devon from its alleged slumbers, aided by the Oxford and Tractarian movements. Bishop Philpott enforced a ritual and discipline higher than the diocese was used to, or liked. Nevertheless, there were still hunting parsons and neglected churches with no-one to tend to them. Philpott took his clergy to court, deserted Exeter for Torquay, and was conspicuously (though possibly una-voidably) absent from the city during the cholera epidemic. He was a con-troversial figure nationally, and his feud with the radical Thomas Latimer, editor of the *Western Times,* was famous.

Roman Catholics, almost but never entirely absent from the diocese since the Reformation, re-established themselves. Buckfast Abbey was begun in 1882, and the Catholic diocese of Plymouth was formed in 1850. The Bridgettine nuns came to Chudleigh in 1887. This did not prevent one of the last of the old Catholic gentry, Arthur Chichester of Arlington Court, from announcing his conversion to the Church of England from the steps of Exeter Cathedral. Strongly-held religious opinions subsided slowly in Devon; the decline of such intense religious feelings was perhaps hastened by the decline in industry and trade, in which dissent had found so much of its strength.

17

The Twentieth Century

Ominously, this century opened with the country at war. Devon was deeply involved in the Boer War. The Commander of the Natal Field Force was General Sir Redvers Buller of Downes near Crediton. To national jubilation, his army relieved the town of Ladysmith, long under siege by the Boers, at the fourth attempt. Inside that town, part of its defence force was the 1st Battalion of the Devon Regiment, whilst the 2nd Battalion was in the relieving column: their meeting was possibly the only occasion on which the two battalions met on campaign, and was to be long remembered.

Twelve years later the country was engaged in a war which was to destroy the old order in Europe, and to speed up a shift in the structure of society in this country which could not fail to affect Devon. Changes were already under way in 1914. By that date elected county councils and parish councils seemed to threaten the supremacy of landed families. The ownership of land no longer carried so much prestige, or assured its possessor of a large income, and this situation was compounded by the introduction of new estate and death duties by the Liberal government in 1906.

A vast acreage of land was put up for sale by the great landlords both before and after the First World War. In Devon, the Duke of Bedford sold most of his land immediately around Tavistock in 1910, and Lord Portsmouth sold the Eggesford estate in 1912. More Bedford land was sold in 1919 and, much more recently, in 1956, a further 9,000 acres was disposed of to pay death duties. Now only one farm remains of all the estates of Tavistock Abbey, acquired by the first Earl of Bedford in Henry VIII's day. Lord Clinton, the inheritor of the vast Rolle estates, sold some 126 farms and 15,000 acres in 1958, and the ugly Rolle mansion of Stevenstone was demolished. The Walronds have left Bradfield, theirs since King John's day; the National Trust was given Killerton by the Aclands, and Arlington by the last of one line of the Chichesters.

147 *The Walrond tomb in Uffculme Church. The Walronds lived at Bradfield in Uffculme from the early 13th to the 20th centuries.*

148 *Copper Castle is a 19th-century castellated tollhouse situated at the eastern end of Honiton on the Axminster Road, seen here still with its road gates.*

It would be wrong, however, to say that the landowner is extinct. Lord Clinton still owns some 18,000-20,000 acres in Devon; the Fortescues 5,000. The Duchy of Cornwall, the Ecclesiastical Commissioners and the National Trust are now landowners on some scale, but in main the great estates were sold to their tenants. Today two-thirds of Devon's land is owned by its occupiers; nearly three-quarters of Devon's farmers own their own farms. In the 19th century less than a fifth was so owned. It is a remarkable social and economic reversal, and with it there has been a shift in influence and power.

The first motor car appeared in Exeter in 1899, and there were 'hundreds' in the city by 1914. 1893 saw the beginnings of the university, and the provision of education by the county council was a subject which attracted interest and controversy. But much had not changed. M.P.s, J.P.s, and county councillors were still largely gentry; folk were still leaving the land and the villages; farm workers were still miserably paid. In Sidmouth, Stephen Reynolds had drawn attention to the plight of another hard-pressed class, the inshore fishermen, in his classics *A Poor Man's House* and *Alongshore*. The 'aged and impotent' poor still found their way into what were until 1931 still 'workhouses', though the introduction of old age pensions in 1908 made this fate less inevitable. Mining was largely dead and, except in Plymouth, there was still little industry. Railways now served the whole county and, for the better-off, Devon was principally seen as an attractive haven for holidays.

The First World War was greeted with enthusiasm: men flocked to the depots of the Devonshire Regiment to enlist. Twelve thousand Devonians were already in the forces. Devon was in no direct danger from German attack; the most visible signs of the war were the mounting casualty lists in the papers, the Belgian refugees who arrived in the city in some numbers, and the creation of at least 25 hospitals all over the county.

At Plymouth the impact of the war was much more direct. The fleet had been mobilised and the reservists, many of them local men, called up before hostilities began. Two Devonport-manned ships were sunk at Coronel, and five more lost at Jutland in 1916 with heavy casualties. A hundred or so fishing smacks were sunk in the Western Channel and, at the height of the U-boat blockade in 1917, 100 merchant ships were sunk around the coasts of Devon and Cornwall, many within sight of the cliffs. The adoption of the convoy system saved the situation, Devonport and Milford Haven both becoming convoy assembly ports.

Initially, civilians only suffered minor shortages, but food was rationed in 1917, wages regulated, and factories taken over for the war effort. Farmers were ordered to plough up grassland for crops; corn acreage in the county went up by 60 per cent in four years. Morale fell as the casualty lists mounted. In May 1918, the Devons lost 518 out of 550 men at Bois des Buttes, stemming the last German push that so nearly came off. For this action the regiment was awarded the Croix de Guerre by the French government. By 1918 very few of its original personnel were still alive, and its original four battalions had grown to sixteen. Small villages like Thelbridge lost 13 men out of a total population of 200 or so, and every village and town has its memorial to those who gave their lives.

149 *The Devon county motif.*

The end of the war was greeted with enthusiasm and hopes of a better life for ordinary folk. But the returning soldiers found little work, and ultimately for many only disillusionment and depression. As in the rest of the country, the Liberal Party was routed, and Devon was now solidly Conservative, except in Plymouth, where the Labour Party established itself strongly. Devon's first Labour M.P., Jimmy Moses, Lord Mayor of Plymouth, was elected in 1929. In the 1930s, in the worst of the depression, Fascist and Communist parties were formed, and rival meetings were held in Fore Street, Exeter, kept apart by the police.

In 1926, during the General Strike, a football match between strikers and police in Plymouth made the national headlines. This apparent sign of basic goodwill was not in fact typical of the true situation. Most Devonshire trade unionists (railwaymen in particular) were solid for the strike, in the face of a hostile press and public opinion. Plymouth unemployment was always above the national average, and the town experienced much labour trouble after the war when the dockyard laid off many workers.

After 1920, with a much smaller landed interest in parliament to protect them, the farmers were abandoned in favour of free trade and cheap food. Those who had bought their farms in post-war euphoria were faced with heavy debts. Farmers with good, fertile land were reduced to taking in guests and trapping rabbits to live. Much of the poorer land reverted to neglected pasture or scrub. Farms were left unlet, or changed hands very cheaply—a situation which benefited some labourers who took farms at a low rent and were eventually able to buy their own properties. Eventually the establishment of the Milk Marketing Board offered the chance of a tolerable income, and milk factories were set up in rural areas.

Many viewed the dereliction of country life with alarm. Amongst them was Leonard Elmhirst, who bought Dartington Hall in 1925. He attempted to create a prosperous rural community, a task made easier by his wife's American wealth. Modern farming and forestry practices were introduced on the Dartington estate; the first artificial insemination centre for cattle was set up, as well as other enterprises, not all with success. The hall itself was turned into one of the most charming complexes of buildings and gardens in the country. The school, founded on what

150 *The badge of the Devonshire Regiment.*

151 *Heinkel III used in bombing raids over Plymouth.*

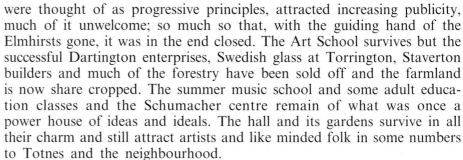

were thought of as progressive principles, attracted increasing publicity, much of it unwelcome; so much so that, with the guiding hand of the Elmhirsts gone, it was in the end closed. The Art School survives but the successful Dartington enterprises, Swedish glass at Torrington, Staverton builders and much of the forestry have been sold off and the farmland is now share cropped. The summer music school and some adult education classes and the Schumacher centre remain of what was once a power house of ideas and ideals. The hall and its gardens survive in all their charm and still attract artists and like minded folk in some numbers to Totnes and the neighbourhood.

For many country folk, visitors provided an essential part of their income. The middle classes had discovered inland Devon, and looked for the spots which had inspired such famous works as Conan Doyle's *Hound of the Baskervilles*, Kipling's *Stalky and Co*, and Henry Williamson's *Tarka the Otter*.

When the Second World War broke out, the beaches were mined and all the estuaries had gun batteries. This time, the county did not pass through the conflict unscathed. Plymouth and Exeter were both heavily bombed. The heart of Plymouth was destroyed between November 1940 and May 1941; in all there were 59 raids on the city, in which some 1,228 tons of bombs were dropped, 1,172 civilians killed, 3,700 houses destroyed and 72,000 damaged. Plymouth was the most heavily-bombed city in England, size for size. Much of the centre of Exeter was burnt out in raids in April and May 1942. On 4 May 10,000 incendiaries were dropped, destroying 1,500 buildings and killing 161 civilians. By a miracle the cathedral largely escaped damage.

Every village had its Home Guard; there were radar stations, the first two being at West Prawle and Hawkstor. By the end of the war there were fighter airfields, Coastal Command fields and a flying boat base. Polish 'Defiant' night fighters and a squadron of Hurricanes were stationed at Exeter, and there were American aircraft at Winkleigh and Dunkeswell. For a year eight villages and six parishes around Slapton Sands were evacuated. The landscape there matched almost exactly the beaches and *bocage* countryside of Normandy. American tanks and infantry took over the area and villagers watched from afar as their homes were bombarded. All this preparation for D-Day eventually culminated in the sailing of the Allied forces from ports all along the south coast, including Dartmouth, Plymouth and the Exe.

After the war, Exeter and Plymouth had to rebuild. Few today wax enthusiastic about the windy, canyon blocks of Armada Way and Royal Parade in Plymouth, though the concept had a certain nobility and is the better for pedestrianisation. Sidwell Street and South Street and the Guildhall Centre in Exeter are little better. Exeter is held by many to be one of the most agreeable cities in which to live; green hills and fields are everywhere visible.

Food was short after the war and, for this reason, farming was not abandoned as it was after the First World War. Corn acreages had in-

152 *Boulton and Paul 'Defiant' night fighter, used by the Polish squadron based at Exeter.*

creased during the war from 136,000 to 326,000 acres, largely with the help
of Devon's 23,000 farm horses. Most villages saw their first tractor in the
late 1930s, but there were still only 6,000 in 1945. By the 1960s the horse
had disappeared from farm life. After the war farming prospered, notably
since the entry into the Common Market. Subsidies, science, and mecha-
nisation have been the agents of this prosperity, coupled with prices set to
ensure that the small less efficient continental farmer got a living. Since
1945 the labour used on the farm has more than halved, but Devon farmers
are keeping more cattle and sheep than ever before. The last decade has
seen milk quotas and 'set aside' land, and most recently the scourge of BSE
and also low prices for milk and meat. Many small farms have disappeared,
swallowed up by larger neighbours, and their farmhouses, often in one
family for generations, have been sold and done up to modern tastes and
detached from their land. Traditional farm buildings are too small for
modern farming and threshing barns and linhays have been converted to
houses in great numbers. This helps to repopulate the countryside, but the
old and the new do not always match well. Much of the countryside is now
being suburbanised with street lights and housing estates.

153 *Modern housing.
Dyers Court, the Shil-
hay, Exeter; built by the
river on an ancient industrial site where cloth had
been dyed for centuries.*

When the war ended folk continued to leave the land and the villages,
but surprisingly, this trend did not continue. A process of 'counter-
urbanisation' was revealed by the censuses. Some young and middle-
aged folk seemed prepared to take a drop in their standard of living in
order to have the peace and quiet of country life. Many villages have
craftsmen again, as well as commuters, telecabins, small factories and
trading estates. The new villagers—teachers, lawyers and businessmen—
are vocal about the loss of village amenities. Many small rural schools
have disappeared, but those that are left have gained in numbers.

Many of the market towns have attracted huge private housing
estates to their outskirts and their accompanying out-of-town
supermarkets. Some town centres are in decline with empty or run down
shops. The seaside resorts have also gone 'down market' as have their
couterparts all over the country. Torquay, 'the queen of English resorts',
in its superb setting still has some grand hotels, but there is a fun fair on
Torre Abbey meadows in summer and the Pavilion is a shopping mall.

Inevitably the Devonshire climate and scenery has attracted those
looking for comfortable retirement. Villages are full of bungalows for the
retired and for commuters to the towns; some disastrous large 'suburban'
estates have been 'planted', as at Feniton and Dunkeswell in east Devon,
in a totally rural setting, detached from any existing social centre. Many
villages have lost their shops and pubs and schools and share a vicar.
Catering for the old is a business; in 1986 there were 464 registered
nursing or retirement homes in the county. The county of the slaver
Hawkins and the East India pilot John Davis has, however, not attracted
many coloured people, though many towns have Indian and Chinese
restaurants. Open moors and commons and wide road verges have
attracted 'new age travellers', but they have difficulty in finding permanent
sites.

Tourism remains a mainstay of the county's economy. Planning—and the National Trust—have at least ensured that the whole coastline is not a rash of bungalows. Devon has drawn heavily on its past. The countryside can be seen and even experienced in theme parks and country parks of all sorts. Almost all the houses of the gentry are either open to the public or converted to institutional use. Devonshire cream is still a delicacy, though it is seldom the unseparated scalded crusted cream of the past.

After the Second World War the only notable industrial growth has been in Plymouth, where by 1999/2000 some 142 new factories had been built, some being American and Japanese-owned. It was French initiative that developed Plymouths ferry links with the continent. Devonport dockyard, that mainstay of Plymouth and south-western employment and economy for three centuries, has been privatised and the naval establishments run down; some of the fine 18th-century dockyard buildings like the Royal Williams Victualling Yard have been sold to become a museum. Elsewhere in Devon, Appledore still builds specialist ships, and sailing and boats must bring in money and some employment. Fishing is subject to disputed quotas, resulting largely from overfishing, and West-Country fishermen have on occasion sold their quotas to Spanish boats. Much fish caught locally is sold abroad.

The gentry and landowners have deserted politics, and local councillors today are farmers, lawyers, businessmen and the retired. The aristocracy now occupy only the honorary roles of lord lieutenant or high sheriff. Exeter and Plymouth have Labour M.P.s and the South-West preserves something of the old Liberal tradition as a Liberal Democrat stronghold.

154 *20th-century local government: County Hall, Exeter, 1957-64.*

From 1914 to 1974 Plymouth was a totally independent county borough, as was Torbay from 1968. In 1974 they became, probably to their regret, part of the county of Devon, only to revert to their independence in 1998. Many towns with their own mayors have really no more than parish council status.

Exeter University was founded just before the Second World War and acquired full university status just after. It has absorbed St Luke's College, the South-West's most prestigious teacher training college, and now has the largest department of education in the country. Plymouth College of Technology has become a university and has absorbed the two teacher training colleges of St Mark and St John in Plymouth and Rolle in Exmouth and Seale Hayne Agricultural College as well.

In 1900 only the favoured few could receive any secondary education at the grammar schools, mostly of ancient foundation. Now most secondary modern and grammar schools have been amalgamated into comprehensive schools with fairly successful results. Far more children pass exams and go on to university or to further education than ever before.

Today there are probably more Roman Catholics in Devon, many of them of Irish descent, than at any time since the Reformation; few towns are without a well accepted catholic church. The Jewish population of Plymouth and Exeter, once numerous and obvious, has been tolerantly assimilated. Many nonconformist chapels have been sold, but many attract loyal and even expanding evangelical congregations. In the Exeter diocese anglican churches are well served and maintained though many parishes have been amalgamated; it is doubtful if the attendance is anything like as high as the 40 per cent of the county's population that attended an anglican service in March 1851.

155 *20th-century communications: the motorway west of Exeter. Before this was built there were regular queues many miles long approaching Haldon Hill.*

It is not easy to be optimistic about the economic future of Devon. There have been no Celtic sea oil finds, the price of tin is too low to keep even one mine at work, though there are enormous reserves in the South-West. Gold is to be mined near Crediton and China clay and ball clay are still extracted in quantity and sold all over the world. Both fishing and farming are depressed. Geography determines that Devon is on the periphery of areas of growth.

The competition of sunnier beaches a short plane's flight away must affect conventional tourism, but Devon has other less obvious attractions to offer in great variety. The county is in general full of good and contrasting scenery, has a wonderful coastline, is quiet, not too crowded, relatively warm, and without major crime, and is for many an immensely attractive place to live and retire to. If it has lost much of its native idiom and rural style and if the Devonshire dialect is now seldom heard—and mocked when it is—that probably does not bother the new Devonians, the incomers who probably now make up the majority. The character of Devon today was set largely in the last hundred and fifty years and is very different from that of the rest of its busy, industrious, troublesome and often hazardous past.

156 *Torquay harbour with coastal shipping.*

157 *Schooners like these plied their trade until the First World War and the advent of motor transport.*

Select Bibliography

Abbreviations:
TDA: Transactions of the Devonshire Association
DAS: Devon Archaeological Society
DCRS: Devon and Cornwall Record Society
EPEH: Exeter Papers in Economic History

Exeter Papers in Economic History: 1. The South West and the Sea; 2. The South West and the Land; 3. Industry and Society in the South West; 4. Ports and Shipping in the South West; 5. Farming and Transport in the South West; 6. Provincial Labour History; 7. Transport and Shipowning in the West Country; 8. Husbandry and Marketing in the South West, 1500-1800; 9. Capital Formation in South West England; 10. Education and Labour in the South West; 11. Population and Marketing in the South West; 12. Reactions to Social and Economic Change, 1750-1939; 13. West Country Maritime and Social History; 14. Agricultural Improvement: Medieval and Modern.

By far the most complete bibliography of Devon history up to 1953 appears in W.G. Hoskins Devon *pp. 554-71.*

A Historical Atlas of South West England eds. Roger Kain and William Ravenhill (1999)
Alcock, N., 'An East Devon Manor in the Middle Ages', *TDA* (1970)
Andriette, E., *Devon and Exeter in the Civil War* (1971)
Barlow, F., ed., *Exeter and its Region* (1969)
Barlow, Frank, 'Hunting in Devon', *TDA* (1981)
Beacham, Peter and Child, Peter, *Devon Buildings* (1990)
Bennet, H.S., *Life on the English Manor* (1948)
Beresford, Maurice, *Medieval New Towns* (1967)
Beresford, Maurice and Finberg, H.P.R., *Handlist of Medieval Boroughs* (1973)
Bidwell, *The Legionary Bath House and Basilica at Exeter* (1979)
Bidwell, Paul, *Roman Exeter* (1980)
Bohstedt, J.H., 'Riots in England with special reference to Devon', unpublished Ph.D. thesis for the University of Harvard, 1972
Booker, Frank, *The Industrial Archaeology of the Tamar Valley* (1971)
Booker, Frank, *The History of the G.W.R.* (1977)
Born, Anne, *The Torbay Towns* (1989)
Born, Anne, *Kingsbridge and Salcombe* (1986)
Bradbeer, G., *The Land Changed its Face: The Evacuation of the South Hams* (1973)
Branigan, K. and Fowler, P.J., *The Roman West Country* (1976)

'British Vessels Lost at Sea, 1914-1918', HMSO (1919)

Burt, Roger, *Devon and Somerset Mines* (1984)

Butler, Jeremy, *An Atlas of Dartmoor Antiquities* (1991)

Carswell, J., *The Descent on England* (1969)

Carus-Wilson, E.M., 'An Industrial Revolution of the Thirteenth Century', *Economic History Review* (1941)

Carus-Wilson, E.M., *The Expansion of Exeter at the Close of the Middle Ages* (1961)

Chapman, Geoffrey, *A History of Axminster* (1998)

Chope, R. Pearce., ed., *Early Tours of Devon and Cornwall* (1918)

Churchwardens' Accounts for Morebath (1904)

Clapp, Brian, *The University of Exeter* (1982)

Clew, Kenneth, *The Exeter Canal* (1984)

Coate, Mary, *Cornwall in the Great Civil War* (1963)

Colepresse, Samuel, 'A georgicalle account of Devon and Cornwall', *TDA* (1964)

Collier, Basil, 'The Defence of the U.K.', *History of the Second World War* (1957)

Cornwall, Julian, *The Revolt of the Peasantry* (1977)

Darby, H.C., *The Domesday Geography of South Western England* (1967)

Devon and Cornwall: A Preliminary Survey (1947)

'Devon Inventories', *DCRS* (1966)

Dunsford, M., *Historical Memoirs of Tiverton* (1790)

Earle, Peter, *Monmouth's Rebels* (1977)

EPEH, Economic History Department, University of Exeter, Nos. 1-14

Farquharson, A., *History of Honiton* (1891)

Fielder, Duncan, *A History of Bideford* (1985)

Finberg, H.P.R., *The Early Charters of Devon and Cornwall* (1963)

Finberg, H.P.R., *Tavistock Abbey* (1969)

Finch, Greg, 'The Case of Devon in an age of Industrialisation, 1840-1914', unpublished Ph.D. thesis for University of Oxford (1984)

Fleming, Andrew, 'Dartmoor Reaves', *DAS* (1979)

Fleming, Guy, *Plymouth, A Pictorial History* (1995)

Forde Johnson, J., *Hill Forts* (1976)

Fox, Aileen, 'The Farway Necropolis', *DAS* (1948)

Fox, Aileen, 'Countisbury and Martinhoe', *DAS* (1966)

Fox, Aileen, *S.W. England* (1973)

Fox, H.S.A., 'The Field Systems of Devon and Cornwall', unpublished Ph.D. thesis for the University of Cambridge (1971)

Fox, H.S.A., 'Field Systems of East and South Devon, part 1', *TDA* (1972)

Fraser, R., *General View of the Agriculture of Devon* (1794)

Freeman, E.A., *The Norman Conquest* (1868)

Freeman, Ray, *A History of Dartmouth* (1983)

Freeman, Ray, *Dartmouth and its Neighbours* (1990)

Gelling, Margaret, *Signposts to the Past* (1997)

Gill, Crispin, *A New History of Plymouth* (1979)

Gover, J.E.B., Mawer, A. and Stenton, F.M., *The English Place-Name Society: Devon* (1931)

Gray, Todd, *The Garden History of Devon* (1995)

Greaves, Tom, 'The Devon Tin Industry, 1450-1750', unpublished Ph.D. thesis for the University of Exeter (1981)

Halliday, Richard Carew, ed., *Survey of Cornwall* (1953)

Hanham, 'Ashburton as a Parliamentary Borough', *TDA* (1966)

Harris, Helen, *Devon's Century of Change* (1998)

Harte, W.J., ed., *Hooker's Exeter* (1926)

Harvey, Hazel, *Exeter Past* (1996)

Hawker, R.S., *Footprints of Former Men* (1870)

Hawkins, M.W.S., *Plymouth Armada Heroes* (1888)

Higham, R.A., 'The Castles of Medieval Devon', unpublished Ph.D. thesis for the University of Exeter (1979)

Hill, D., *An Atlas of Anglo-Saxon History* (1981)

Hooke, Della, *Pre-conquest charter boundaries of Devon* (1994)

Hooker, John, 'Synopsis Chorographical of Devonshire, 1599', *TDA* (1915)

Sir Ralph Hopton's Narrative (1902)

Hoskins, W.G., *Industry, trade and people in Exeter* (1935)

Hoskins, W.G. and Finberg, H.P.R., *Devonshire Studies* (1952)

Hoskins, W.G., *Devon* (1953)

Hoskins, W.G., *The Making of the English Landscape* (1955)

Hoskins, W.G., *Two Thousand Years in Exeter* (1960)

Hoskins, W.G., *Provincial England* (1963)

Hoskins, W.G., *The Westward Expansion of Wessex* (1970)

Jarvis, K., 'The M5 Motorway', *DAS* (1975)

Lambert, R.S., *The Cobbett of the West* (1939)

Lewis, G.R., *The Stannaries* (1924)

Lysons, Daniel, *Devonshire* (1822)

MacCaffrey, W., *Exeter, 1540-1640* (1975)

Macaulay, Lord, *History of England* (pop. ed. 1895)

MacDermot, E.T., *History of the Forest of Exmoor* (1972)

Macdonald Wigfield, W., *The Monmouth Rebellion* (1980)

Mahotière, Mary de la, *Tiverton* (1990)

Maitland, H.M., *Domesday Book and Beyond* (1906)

Marshall, W., *The Rural Economy of the West of England* (1796)

Memoirs of Colonel Ludlow (1897)

Matthews, Edmund Calamy, ed., *Account of Ministers ejected 1660-1662* (1934)

Meller, Hugh, *Exeter Architecture* (1989)

Miles, Henrietta, 'Roman villa at Honeyditches, Seaton', *Britannia* (1977)

Milles, Jeremiah, MSS. in Bodleian Library, *c*.1755, microfilm in West Country Studies Library

Minchinton, W.E., *Devon at Work* (1974)

Morgan, F.W., 'Domesday Geography of Devon', *TDA* (1940)

Morris, John, *The Age of Arthur* (1977)

Morris, John (gen. ed.) *Domesday Book: Devon*, edited by Caroline and Frank Thorn (1985)

Newton, Robert, *Eighteenth Century Exeter* (1984)

Newton, Robert, *Nineteenth Century Exeter* (1984)

Oliver, G., *Monasticon Diocesis Exoniensis* (1889)

Oppenheim, M., *The Maritime History of Devon* (1968)

Ordericus Vitalis (1853)

Pearce, Susan, *The Kingdom of Dumnonia* (1978)

Pearce, Susan, *The Archaeology of South Western England* (1981)

Pettit, Paul, *Prehistoric Dartmoor* (1974)

Pollard, Sheila, 'Roman villa at Holcombe, Uplyme', *DAS* (1974)

Polwhele, Richard, *History of Devonshire, 1797* (1811)

Price, D.G., 'The Moorland Plym', *TDA* (1979)

Report of the Committee of the Economy of the South West (1965)

'Return of the Owners of Land', HMSO (1873)

Risdon, Tristram, *Chorographical Description of the County of Devon, 1630* (1897)

Roberts, George, *History of Lyme Regis* (1834)

The Chronicle of Roger of Wendover (1841)

Rose-Troup, Frances, *The Prayerbook Rebellion* (1913)

Round, J.H., *Feudal England* (1895)

Rowse, A.L., *Tudor Cornwall* (1969)

Russell, Percy, *Dartmouth* (1950)

Sellman, R.R., *Illustrations of Devon History* (1962)

Sellman, R.R., *Devon Village Schools* (1967)

Seward, David, 'The Devon Cloth Industry in the Early Seventeenth Century', *EPEH* No. 3 (1970)

The Seymour Papers (for the Civil War in the South Hams), Devon Record Office

Silvester, R.A., 'Prehistoric settlement at Dainton', *DAS* (1980)

Snell, L., *The Suppression of the Religious Foundations in Devon and Cornwall* (1967)

Sprigge, Joshua, *'Anglia Rediviva'—an account of the New Model Army* (1647)

Stephens, W.B., *Seventeenth Century Exeter* (1958)

Stoyle, Mark, *Loyalty and Locality* (1994)

Storey, R.L., *The End of the House of Lancaster* (1966)

Susser, Bernard, *The Jews of South West England* (1993)

Taylor, Christopher, *Village and Farmstead* (1983)

The buildings of England. Devon. eds. Bridget Cherry, Nikolaus Pevsner, Judy Nairn and John Newman (1989)

The New Maritime History of Devon eds. Michael Duffy, Stephen Fisher, Basil Greenhill, David J. Starkey and Joyce Youings (1992)

Thomas, D. St J., *Railways in the South West* (1960)

Thompson, F.M.L., *English Landed Society in the Nineteenth Century* (1963)

Trump, H.J., *West Country Harbour* [Teignmouth] (1968)

The Uffculme Archive Group, *Uffculme, A Peculiar Parish* (1997)

Ugawa, K., 'The Economic Development of Some Devon Manors', *TDA* (1962)

Underdown, D., *Somerset in the Civil War* (1973)

Vancouver, C., *The Agriculture of Devon* (1808)

Victoria County History of Devon, vol. 1 (1906)

Walker, John, *The Suffering of the Clergy in the Diocese of Exeter* (1908)

Warne, A., *Church and Society in Eighteenth Century Devon* (1969)

Wasley, Gerald, *Devon at War* (1994)

Westcote, T., *View of Devonshire in 1630* (1845)

Whitelock, Dorothy, ed., *The Anglo-Saxon Chronicle* (1961)

Whitham, John A., *Ottery St Mary* (1984)

Whiting, Roger, *The Blind Devotion of the People* (1989)

Wolffe, B.P., *Henry VI* (1981)

Youings, Joyce, 'Devon Monastic Lands', *DCRS* (1955)

Youings, Joyce, *Tuckers' Hall* (1968)

Youings, Joyce, 'The South Western Rebellion of 1549', *Southern History* (1979)

Young, Michael, *The Elmhirsts of Dartington* (1982)

Zeuner, F.E., 'Tornewton Cave and Chapel', *DAS* and *TDA* (1960)

Index

References to illustrations in the text are indicated by bold type in the index. Colour plates are indicated by Roman numerals.

Making a resort. Building a sea wall at Paignton in 1855.